Ego Alchemy

Journey from the lead of ego to the Gold of Soul

by

Matilda Faltyn

The moral right of the author has been asserted.

This book is copyright. Apart from any fair use for the purposes of private study, research or review, as permitted under the Copyright Act, no part of this book may be reproduced by any process without prior written permission. Inquiries should be addressed through the author's website www.matildafaltyn.com.

Disclaimer

Some names have been changed to protect the identity of real persons.

Due to the dynamic nature of the Internet, any Web addresses or links contained in the Notes section of this book may have changed since publication and may no longer be valid.

Table of Contents

A Note to the Reader

In this time of awakening in the 21st century, we can reclaim our forgotten inner strengths and put them to good use in our personal lives. Even if we can't change the world we can at the very least have a sense of the reality of our world that will not be so absolute, one-sided and fear-based. We can be free in our hearts and minds because we know better with certainty, not just hope.

There are many great spiritual works available from different perspectives, old and new, but they can seem not readily adaptable to everyday life in today's world. The hope behind this book is to bring spirituality and its psychology into ordinary daily life in a lasting sense so it's not so easily shelved as a pet subject or thought of as a lifestyle for fringe-dwelling spiritual boffins.

In Chapter 1, I felt it necessary to share with you my background to all this so you can see where I am coming from. It's been a discovery that came about from an idle curiosity. The simple mind exercises and tips were all tried and tested and are short and easy. But don't be deceived; they work! and they uncover something important that has been systematically concealed from us. The human mind is powerful and we can shape our personal reality to a great extent. Not overnight, mind you, but steadily and surely.

You'll find Ego Alchemy most effective if you start from the beginning of the book and read each chapter in sequence, then refer to selected parts once you are familiar with the contents. Transmuting the lead of ego into the gold of soul is a journey by stages.

Onward and upward,

Matilda Faltyn
March 2015

Website: www.matildafaltyn.com

Introduction and Book Overview

Growing up and living in this world we are encouraged to believe we have only one life. This one life springs up from nowhere and goes back to nothing. At the end of this one life, we die and that is the end of us. At best, a religious person believes that after death comes some form of judgement and a vague notion called 'the soul' is either saved or condemned.

The other belief (not atheist or religious), says that after death we return to the cosmic soup or collective consciousness as an ingredient of nature or life force. Our energy then randomly appears again in another form and place. So with only one life, and no particular reason for being here, and no lasting identity, we are easily influenced by external controls in whatever form they take. While we live this 'one life' it's hard not to carry more fear than we need for our survival.

We are encouraged to believe the brain is just another organ in the body that merely gets information about the world around us through the five physical senses. That mind and brain are inseparable; that we are no more than meat and bone. We are encouraged to believe that mild mental instability or illness should be treated with prescription drugs and other invasive forms of treatment – that a person can't learn and isn't able to discipline or control their own mind.

These notions are entrenched by our popular culture which is completely geared to the ego and keeps us operating at well below our capacity. The ego is well equipped to survive in the three dimensional world bound by linear time and space. I am not sure if we were fitted with it, or if it grew out of the environment we live from the necessity of surviving in a physical world. I have a feeling it's the latter. The problem is that we are so hypnotised by the daily routine, commitments, and pace of living this one life, that ego has come to dominate our conscious awareness and conceals the true self which is our eternal soul.

Because the nature of the soul is not explained in education or religion in a way that shows it's real, it makes the soul seem abstract – an old-fashioned concept that doesn't fit into our modern containers. It seems to belong to an era when people believed in ghosts and haunted houses. Because it's not well defined we have almost forgotten we have a soul.

For a long time I was buffeted by external controls, I put up with my moods and had too many irrational fears. Things seemed to happen to me, I didn't make them happen, so it was easy to feel like a victim when circumstances didn't go my way. In this sense I was an average person and never thought or even suspected there might be a better way of being. But for a couple of turning points in my life, I could still be in that mental place.

This awakening to our real soul nature is within reach for anyone. What's striking about my story is how ordinary it is. No phoenix-like rising from the ashes of some gut-wrenching tragedy or abuse, or being born with 'gifts', or having exclusive contact with ascended masters. To find the gold of soul, after spending so much of my life living under the limits of my leaden ego, is a story that must be shared.

With personal experiences and real life dialogues (peppered throughout the book), and an array of easy mind exercises that were tried and tested, I hope to demonstrate that spirituality is more than a philosophy. I also share wisdoms from teachings by well-known and obscure spiritual teachers and authors.

So to see what's in store, here is an outline of the chapters...

Chapter 1 – The Starting Point

- If you think spirituality is only a philosophy, you are not alone. Many of us are raised in a family religion only to doubt it in young adulthood. I came to a point when I started to question reality at a time mainstream religion was losing followers.

- After stumbling upon an ancient religion, I studied and practised with the religious group for several years. Then I left it after having doubts about parts of their teachings that seemed cult-like.

- While treading water spiritually, I met another person who turned out to be also on a spiritual quest. We made friends and started a dialogue.

Chapter 2 - The Ego Self

- Is there is a difference between ego and soul? Assuming the soul is real, and the ego is fabricated, let's consider a possible origin of ego by using the

Christian biblical story of Adam and Eve's fall from grace from the Garden of Eden as a metaphor. It seems to represent the sinking of the soul and the domination of ego.

- In the early 20th century, psychologists Freud and Jung developed theories about the human personality and found experiential evidence for the soul and the ego. Their work paved the way for New Age understanding of ego as well as the discovery of a super-conscious.

- To gain a holistic view of how ego is different from the soul, we compare the psychological and the spiritual understandings of ego.

Chapter 3 – Ego Anatomy

- What is ego made of and how does it take over a person? It's essentially an array of fear-based and conflicting emotions. A closer look at the geography of ego reveals how to spot it in yourself mentally, emotionally and physically. How ego can complicate and make life harder than it needs to be, and holds a person back.

- The generally known Christian understanding of ego is the Catholic Seven Deadly Sins concept which is matched against the conquering virtues. For each vice there is a virtue, so you can see how an ego vice can transmute into a soul virtue.

- The ancient Christian understanding of ego is even more useful. Presenting the Gnostic Five Inferior

Centres (in the body) it's possible to perceive when ego manipulates us like a puppet on a string.

- Using a dialectic approach to question three Gnostic ideas about ego and consciousness, I was able to make sense of the doubts I had about some of the teachings.

Chapter 4 – Ego Psychology

- After reconciling the ideas about ego so far, there is now a way to forge ahead with how to handle the ego (the little self, doppelganger – or however you want to cast your ego in relation to your true self, the soul).

- Ego thoughts take you out of the present moment. There are ways to manage your thoughts so the tail no longer wags the dog. Understand the feedback loop between thoughts and feelings and how to avoid slipping into moods and repetitive thinking.

- Ego doesn't like challenge or change. When you face these times ego will create self-limiting thoughts. It can be bad enough to make a person indecisive, then a stalemate leads to inaction. How many great ideas never saw the light of day because of this syndrome.

- Ego thinks it's pitted against everyone else in the world in a competition for the goodies of life. It encourages barriers between people through false impressions, misunderstandings, and jumping to conclusions. It's like a hall of mirrors and drains your energy. It divides and conquers within a person and without a person (among others).

Chapter 5 – Ego in Training

- This is where the rubber hits the road, but instead of having to take time out or making the time for ego alchemy, it's simply a matter of integrating a new awareness into your daily life.

- Develop an understanding of your personal boundary and how to apply it in relation to others. This is vital for very sensitive or empathic people who pick up vibes from others and have trouble telling which feelings and impressions are their's or someone else's.

- There are general tips for keeping ego in check and staying positive when the going gets tough. There are two arenas in life where we are tested mercilessly by ego – in work and with family.

- When I was going through a difficult time in my life I resorted to naming my ego faces that were bothering me the most. It turned out to be a very useful (and fun) exercise as I was able to quarantine the parts of my ego that were increasing my suffering.

Chapter 6 – Situational Ego Training Exercises

- Ego is not a person you can confine to a space or make a booking with for some one-on-one coaching because ego is master at pretenses and as slippery as an eel.

- If you have tried the exercise of naming your ego faces, you'll have a roll call of your own ego faces that you can focus on to train one at a time whenever there is an opportunity.

- There are ten ego training exercises which address the common negative ego trips and difficult situations a person can face in their life. When you train your ego situationally, by using everyday happenings as they arise, it becomes a spontaneous effort and ego has no time to put on its various masks to hide from you.

Chapter 7 – Mentoring your Ego

- Once ego is aware of your new awareness, the time is ripe for a more advanced way of training it. Being a mentor to your ego means you're not in opposition to it but can work together in a beneficial way.

- Looking at the shadow side of ego, it's possible to gain a deeper insight into your psyche. Shining light on it releases some of the suppressed potential that's been blocked and locked away. Two exercises are presented to open the heart and let go of past emotional pain.

- I reveal a major ego challenge I went through and how I coped. From this experience I learned more about my shadow side and experimented with a mind exercise to tap into this murky reservoir.

- It's shadow that produces 'counter intentions' when the law of attraction or positive thinking fails to manifest personal goals. It's those out of touch parts of us that derail or sabotage our efforts. It can be a good thing or a bad thing.

- The 'power of silence' when used, gives soul a chance to take centre stage (for a change) at those times when you could use some inspiration. It is a strength that can save you from wasting your energy. We look at some everyday situations that demonstrate this strength when dealing with others.

- Finally, after so much work on yourself, you may feel back at square one when dealing with other people's egos. Ways of dealing with heightened sensitivities and intolerances are presented.

Chapter 8 – Being Your Higher self (the soul)

- The eternal soul has also been known as the 'small still voice'. It is fearless, potent, creative, inspirational and invincible. When you are fully present in the moment you can feel your higher self as a conscious awareness.

- It is possible to recognise your higher self, or soul, and tap into it through self awareness. Communication with your soul is always valuable. An exercise to open the heart intelligence and connect with your soul is presented.

- 'Being in the Now' as a general habit is the most direct way to connect with your soul or higher self. Cultivating the ability to be fully present in the moment (as often as you remember) has some surprising benefits.

- There are mantra chanting exercises to massage the chakras in the body. Use mantras and affirmations to nourish your mind and body and tap into your inner wisdom. Three examples of tapping into the higher self to solve everyday situational problems are presented.

- Getting wisdom and help from your soul is a matter of tuning in and being receptive. There are ways to increase your receptivity.

- Two spiritual qualities of the soul are discussed using real life situations. We also look at how to encourage these qualities and what's to gain by harnessing them.

Chapter 9 – Spiritual Discernment

- You can tell when you are in that state of readiness for a spiritual quest into the gold of soul. It's got to be more than a passing curiosity for lasting results.

- Be discerning when you start to investigate spirituality. Discover some good rules of thumb and advice (born from experience) on how to discern genuine spiritual truths in books, schools of thought, and psychics. Increase your ability to tell the difference between truth and fake.

- Dealing with spiritual readiness in the context of your life might come into play if change happens from within and radiates out and others in your life are curious about the change in you, or sceptical about your new interest.

- How it feels to be operating more from your higher self and the benefits you gain. The journey wraps up with an encounter I shared with my spiritual friend that showed the lead of ego and the gold of soul in action.

Ego alchemy in a sense is not new. In the 1930s the famous economist, John Maynard Keynes, bought the personal papers of the scientist, Isaac Newton, at an auction. Keynes was surprised to discover from these papers that Newton secretly experimented with alchemy. There was a side to alchemy that was less talked about and inspired Newton the most. It was the search for the Philosopher's Stone - the prospect of discovering the 'elixir of life'. It really means changing the base metal of the leaden ego into the gold of soul.

I hope you enjoy your journey of discovery in Ego Alchemy.

Chapter 1: The Starting Point

I started my spiritual journey by chance. I never intended to go back to religion or find God when I got to a certain age. When I was a young adult, I thought that to be spiritual you had to deny pleasure and submit to a higher authority. I was sure it meant giving up your individuality and merging with a collective consciousness like a brick in the wall. So I avoided spirituality for most of my young adult life. I didn't want to abstain from anything. I wanted to be bold and cheeky and make mistakes. The last thing I wanted was a dogma riddled with rules.

There are stories of people who became spiritual after suffering a terrible tragedy or severe and awful abuse. This could give the impression that you have to be desperate to be spiritual. This is not the case with me; my experiences were not gut-wrenching but they were strange and out of place enough for me to feel doubt about what I understood to be real. I have this in common with the vast majority of people who do not have extreme life stories to tell, and who probably feel their point of view lacks shock appeal and so remain silent.

They say the ages of seven to nine are formative and very impressionable. The roots of my spiritual awakening started from experiences I had in that age. What they did was make me introverted and uncertain about basic things we take for granted – like the rightness of authority and the sanctity of the family home. To a child, life revolves around home and school, and it was in these two arenas that my sensibilities were rattled.

Early Doubts

My parents and I migrated to Australia from Poland in 1962 – I was a baby, my father was a carpenter, and my mother a shop assistant. My parents were an odd couple, my mother was more of a listener than a talker, and my father would brood a lot. They hardly spoke to each other and home life would switch between mausoleum silence and the sudden explosive angry rantings of my father after he'd had too many drinks.

The only time I'd have a conversation with my father was to argue with him about access to the TV. As an only child, I escaped the loneliness by reading lots of books, wonderful books that took me away. I could see my parents struggling with cultural differences while trying to learn English as quickly as possible. When my father drank too much (which was nearly every day) he sometimes broke things like glass, crockery and furniture which he started to do when I was four.

I never forgot one time when I was about nine years old. He went on a rampage through the whole house and my mother and I had to flee to our neighbours who put us up for the night. The next morning, when we returned home, the inside was a shambles with overturned and broken furniture, shattered glass and debris. It looked like a tornado had ripped through our home.

Around this time, an unfortunate coincidence occurred about a month after my father's rampage through the house. Because both my parents worked, I was a latchkey kid. I was the first one home so I had my own house key and would let myself in. One summer afternoon after school, I was walking home along the suburban streets of red brick bungalow houses. A thunder storm was brewing. The clouds were so dark the street lights came on. Fat rain drops started to pelt down so I ran the rest of the way home.

When I got home and opened the front door, panting and wet, I was stunned to find the inside completely messed up with furniture overturned and objects broken and scattered everywhere. Bewildered, I quickly concluded that wild dogs must have run riot through our home. There was food smashed and smeared all over the walls. Coffee, tea, sugar and flour were spilled all over the kitchen floor in patterns. On my bedroom wall was a large graffiti of Mr Foo. The only semblance of order was a piece of human poo coiled neatly in the cup of an ashtray in the lounge room. I slowly sat down on the couch and waited for my father to come home and thought about the wild dogs. The police came and went but the burglars were never caught.

In my primary school years, in the early 1970s, I went to a Catholic school which was on a main road in the inner western suburbs of Sydney. The church at the front had very high Roman columns at the entrance. It looked like it had been plucked from an old part of Italy and dropped in the bland landscape of Australian suburbia. Most of the nuns at St Joseph's Primary School were patient and kind except for one I had in Year 6 - an old Irish nun called Sister Patrick. She was old and strict, disciplinarian, and always sour.

In those days they still used corporal punishment in schools so it was normal to get the cane for misbehaviour. The cane stick was used like a whip to strike it across the fingers of your outstretched hand, but Sister Patrick liked to administer it with the palm of the child's hand facing down. I remember when two girls from Year 4 were called in to stand in front of us all to receive the cane. When the girls went back to their class, there was a puddle on the floor where they had been standing. With a face like sauerkraut, Sister Patrick mopped it up muttering her disgust.

It seemed like a decent education except for the religious part. We had to study the Catechism, the official Catholic textbook that reads like a legal document. We said prayers six times a day and went to confession once a month. Confession took place in a double cubicle in the church which was partitioned with a small veiled window that separated the priest from the child so you couldn't see the priest's face. The priest would listen to the child's confession, then tell the child what prayers to say to repent, called penance. The child would go back to the pew seats and say their penance quietly before going back to class.

My friends and I had a routine with the confession and that was to tell the same two sins every time. The sins were, 'I have told lies' and 'I have been disobedient.' Every single month we went with this format which received a penance of five Hail Marys. One month I thought I would add a little variety, so I included a third sin and that was, 'I have been lazy.'

Well I felt very put out when the priest also broke with the routine and gave me a penance of twenty Hail Marys. I felt uncomfortable like I must be bad. I went back to the pew and started to pray. When I finished the seventh Hail Mary, I looked around the church and saw that I was completely alone. My child's logic could have been flawed, but this didn't sit right with me. How can the whole of my class be finished so quickly? I left the church without finishing my penance. That was the first time I started to feel doubt about religion and authority.

Search for Meaning

As a young adult in the 1980s and 1990s, I was agnostic (doubting that the existence of God can be known, or whether God exists at all). It was a time when many were openly questioning the value of organised religion. Young people, especially, were losing faith as the rising star of information technology and science brought new paradigms about reality, like Chaos Theory. It seemed that science would eventually provide all the answers since religion hadn't advanced at all compared with the scientific discoveries about the nature of our physical universe.

Even so, I always thought maths and science were the alphabet and tools of creation so at times I wondered about the meaning of life beyond scientific answers. Usually it was an inner dialogue along the lines of: why does anything exist at all, why is there a universe populated with life? The answer that would pop into my mind was 'because Nature abhors a vacuum'. This phrase was coined by the ancient philosopher Aristotle who observed that nature requires every space to be filled with something.

Then who or what is Nature, I would wonder. Is it a life force? To be a force that produces living things, there must be a certain amount of consciousness or will. It's not enough to say life simply follows biological, physical and chemical laws. There's more to living than mechanical existence. There is conscious existence and the joy of living. We've seen warm-blooded animals play in a way that looks like they know how to enjoy themselves. It's clear they are more than just flesh and bones mechanically functioning to survive. It looked to me like science was not ready to do away with God just yet.

One of the social issues that was debated in the 1990s was that mainstream religion was losing members and not attracting young people. In 1997, the Australian public television station, ABC, broadcast an open discussion forum called *Has the Church Lost its Way?*[1] It invited three representatives from the main Christian religions: Catholic, Uniting Church, and Anglican. The presenter opened the discussion in front of a small studio audience of interest groups and members of the public. I was so impressed with the way this topic was handled that I bought the program on video which I still have today.

The presenter started with a few statistical facts. The population census between 1901 and 1991 showed a steady decline in church attendance from 91 percent of the population to under 60 percent, with the sharpest drop between the 1950s and 1970s.[2] A young woman in the audience, who was waiting to be ordained into priesthood in the Uniting Church, made a very good point: that more people in the past went to church because it was the done thing. Now the people that go today are those who actually want to be there.

It was generally agreed that churches which continue to grow are those who try to stay relevant to modern life. During the 1980s, fringe and evangelical churches attracted young people because they seemed more emotionally expressive and were passionate about a 'living faith'. The young were not only looking for richer answers to the meaning of life, but to connect faith with daily living that can make a difference in the world. If that meant changing sermons to discussions, church pews to round tables, and teachers instead of preachers, then so be it.

Another emerging sensibility was that important social movements in society do not need an institution to grow. The Anglican priest thought this was more idealistic than realistic, but he could not deny there was 'a deep longing for meaning' (as he put it) that was not being satisfied by mainstream religion.

How Religious Faith Survived

The questioning about the relevance of organised religion for future generations influenced the education system in the years to come. After I had my daughter in 2000 and became involved in her school and her learning, I discovered the study of religion was modernised. While my daughter's school was not religious, it has Anglican roots and they taught Religious Education as a non-core subject. I joined the school's Parent Prayer Group out of curiosity where I met the Religious Education teacher who was peachy-faced and enthusiastic about the subject.

The teaching materials have changed. They are written in conversational style that students can read without going cross-eyed. Cartoon strips are used to tell a biblical story and puzzles to solve religious themes. There was more use of worksheets with engaging questions so students could think for themselves about what God and faith mean to them. Instead of being dictated to, students were asked to think about how religious ideals could be applied in every day life. In England, some schools have stopped teaching religion as an isolated subject and renamed it Social & Religious Studies.

Today, I am surprised by the resiliency of religious faith and that young people who are involved do so out of choice. There is a new appreciation for the many religious traditions in the world with the merging of Eastern and Western thinking. Many long buried and forgotten spiritual truths are being rediscovered.

Even though I used to think there was little difference between religion and spirituality, my own research found they can buttress each other. Unlike religion, spirituality is internalised, totally individual and deeply personal. It creates a more global awareness of the unity of all peoples because it's non-denominational and all inclusive. Spirituality suggests that all life is intelligent, conscious, and that there is a higher purpose to existence. Religion is following a faith whereas spirituality is a truth that is perceived, experienced, tested and applied. The positive side of religion is that it binds people in a local community with fellowship, tradition, and good works.

I still felt religion was not for me, but I couldn't help noticing the revival of old spirituality based on ancient mystical and pagan sects. Now to admit that my spiritual starting point was with a heresy is a bit uncomfortable for me. More so because the group I was involved with have since been accused of being a cult by some disgruntled ex-members who have blogged on the internet to denounce them.

All I can say is that life can be full of opposites. Good things can come in bad wrapping, and, bad things can come in good wrapping. How many times have you bought a product (or seen a movie) that had glamorous and very slick packaging only to find the contents didn't live up to the promise. Well the packaging around Gnostic Christianity that I came upon was black and white and had no pretty pictures, but I was more interested in substance at that stage.

Finding Wisdom in a Heresy

Modern research has shown the first traces of Gnostic thought can be found a few centuries before the Christian Era.

It was heavily influenced by Greek Platonic philosophy and the Greek mysteries. It was also synthesised from Asian, Babylonian, Egyptian, and Syrian pagan religions.

My introduction to Gnosticism started one day in 2004 when I saw a plain billboard poster in a suburban shopping arcade. It was about a free lecture on *Astral Travel and Dreams* by a group called the Gnostic Movement. I decided to go out of curiosity as I was always interested in dreams. Although I had a vague idea of what the subject of astral travel was about, I decided if the lecture was too wacky I would get up and leave. Before I describe my experience with this first lecture, let's take a look at the origin of Gnosticism and why the orthodox Christian church branded it a heresy.

The Lost Gnostic Gospels were discovered in December 1945, in the upper Egyptian city of Nag Hammadi. A young Arab peasant was digging for soil to fertilize his crops when he exposed a metre-high red earthenware jar. He hesitated before opening it for fear of uncorking an evil spirit or jin. As he stared at it, curiosity got the better of him, and because the seal couldn't be opened, he smashed the jar. Amongst the rubble, he found thirteen leather-bound papyrus books dating from about 350 AD. They were in remarkably good condition and contained unknown works written in Coptic text.

The site was excavated and 52 texts were eventually recovered. Over several years of intrigue involving illegal sales, smuggling, and academic rivalry, the Gnostic Gospels of St Thomas and Mary Magdalene, among others, were circulated among theology scholars. The complete collection, released as

The Nag Hammadi Library, was not made available in English format until 1977.

The loss of the gospels originated in the 4th century when the Roman Emperor, Constantine, convened a group of bishops to form the Council of Nicaea. In 325 AD, he gave the Council authority to standardise all the Christian schools of thought into an official Christian Church. Since Constantine was the first Christian emperor, it was his hope to make Christianity the uniting ideology of his rule. It was the Council's job to sift through the variety of Christian teachings circulating at the time.

The Gnostic Gospels were written around the same time as the Gospels of the New Testament. Yet they were banned by the Council even though Gnosticism was one of the three main branches of early Christianity in the 200-year period after Jesus' death. The other two branches were the remains of the Jewish Christian sect founded by Jesus' disciples based in Jerusalem, and the churches started by Paul. It was the latter that was allowed to grow and develop into the mainstream Christianity we know today.

By 350 AD, Gnosticism was well and truly edged out of mainstream Christianity. From the orthodox Christian point of view, Gnosticism was not monotheistic. In the Gospel of Philip, one of the banned gospels, it says the heavens are a series of emanations (astral layers?) from the divine source and that our world was created by an intermediary being, not by God. In other words, a lesser god created the material world. This lesser god wanted to create it imperishable and immortal but fell short of the goal.

Is it a coincidence that the Bible refers to the fall of the archangel Lucifer in the New Testament's 1 Timothy 3:6 saying that pride caused his downfall? Legend has it that Lucifer was so proud he declared, 'Better to rule on earth, than serve in heaven'. The Old Testament also describes a fallen angel in Isaiah 14:12-14 and Ezekiel 28:12-18.

In Gnosticism's heyday, there were different schools of thought and each had their own leader. The Valentinian School, the largest and most popular of the time, believed the true God of consciousness was a dyad of the masculine and feminine principles – very much like the yin and yang of the Chinese Tao. This sat well with me as I wondered why we refer to God as 'our Father' and not the Almighty One or Creator, or some other gender-neutral term. Surely, you can't have a father without a mother.

The main reasons Gnosticism was rejected were practical, while others were ideological:

- Gnostics believed that since our physical world was created imperfectly by a lesser god, it was therefore evil and corrupt. Over the ages, this belief justified the labelling of Gnosis as Gnostic Luciferianism. If a lesser god made the physical universe, then it can be none other than Satan.

- Gnostics said that Jesus was a spirit and not actually of the flesh. Both Gnosticism and Christianity say Jesus was born of the Holy Spirit - which is vaguely represented as a white dove in modern Christianity. In Gnosticism, the Holy Spirit is defined as the feminine, or female aspect of God.

- Gnostics place more importance on intuiting the truth through inner knowing. It's not just a detached learning of facts, but a knowing by experience and participation. If we translate this approach in today's terms, we realise it's impossible to comprehend God solely through the intellect. Instead, we can use our latent senses, like perception, intuition, emotions, and capacity for love.

- Gnostics believe in the 'Divine spark' inside every human being (the source of inner knowing). They said this spark can be fanned into a flame which liberates the human soul from the matrix of the physical world. The meaning of the crucifixion of Jesus was not as a human sacrifice to save us from our sins, but to set an example of doing away with the ego, symbolised by His physical body nailed to the cross.

Today, one of the most respected and published Gnostic scholars, Elaine Pagels, says that Christ's death was not meant to be a sacrificial offering.[3] The Gospel of Truth (another banned Gnostic gospel) sees the crucifixion as a metaphor for the discovery of the divine self within. The crucifixion was an extremely dramatic way to portray that meaning, but perhaps it is what made the message unforgettable over the ages.

It's interesting to note the origin of the word 'heresy'. It comes from the Greek word *hairesis* which means choosing, or faction. The influence of early Christianity was expanding throughout the Mediterranean Basin and was not welcomed by the Judean and Roman cultures. In this social and political backdrop, the original meaning of heresy was subverted to mean a serious crime. The various Christian schools circulating at that time each had different ideas about Christ, God, and salvation - many of them controversial.

Lifting the Lid on Modern Gnosticism

From the mid-20th century, several schools and research organisations on Gnosticism emerged. There were two which I became involved with through study and participation. They are the Gnostic Institute of Anthropology and the Gnostic Movement. The Institute is focused on theory and history whereas the Movement is a break-away from the sole focus on theory and has evolved more practical knowledge for use in self development. It was the Movement that intrigued me as I didn't want to just learn intellectually, I wanted to experience the truth.

When I read the poster on the Gnostic Movement's lecture on Astral Travel and Dreams, I was unaware there was a Gnostic presence in Australia. In the past I had heard of Gnosticism but thought the subject was ancient history and not much more. I was intrigued to find a modern rendition of this body of knowledge.

The Gnostic lecture was held in a community centre hall which was newly built and had an open breezy feel thanks to the large windows, light and portable furniture, and dimmable lighting. There were about 60 people of various ages. As I waited for the speaker to arrive I noticed a quietness in the room. I wondered if most people came by themselves (like me) and were self-conscious about being at a place on a subject that was out of the norm.

I looked around to see what types would be attracted to this subject. There were some like me, close to middle-age and dressed casually. Others looked a bit arty and wore trendier fashion with costume jewellery and bleached hair. Some looked like they'd come straight from work, dressed in office clothes, but none too formal. Others looked academic, wearing reading glasses and carrying a pouch of books and papers and balancing loose items like mobile phone and keys. The age range seemed to be between twenties to forties.

When the Gnostic teacher entered, he looked over the room, and smiled giving a warm welcome. I was relieved that he looked like a normal young university student, clean cut and casually dressed. He introduced himself as Jason, a teacher at the Gnostic Movement. He spoke matter-of-factly about the dream life, how we all dream even though we don't always remember, and how we leave our physical bodies at night and enter the fifth dimension of the astral world in our astral body. It would seem there was more to dreams than just mental replays of the day.

Even though I was new to the subject of the astral and didn't know what to make of it, the way Jason approached faith, God and the getting of wisdom, attracted me. He said the only truth is that which you can perceive and experience, and know in your heart. That you had to investigate the teachings for yourself rather than take their word for it. He placed great importance on 'direct experience'. The truth is not something you just read about and memorise, it is felt and experienced. This was irresistible to me. This was not like anything I had ever heard before.

What struck me was that he was talking about this most unusual subject like it was totally normal – no conspiratorial tone or special emphasis in his voice. I think it mesmerised the audience as I am sure many expected a bit of the hard sell with some gesturing or theatrics to try to win (or bamboozle) them over. But no, Jason was almost 'take it or leave it' with his delivery.

He also said that to reach your full potential with Gnostic work you have to be sincere. If you try to force yourself, by sticking to rules, you'll become mechanical, not genuine, and even develop a resistance to your self-improvement efforts. I had never heard common sense like that before.

The subsequent lectures were to be held in another location, their Study Centre. I turned up the next week at the new address to find the so-called study centre was a two-storey terrace house in a residential street. I was taken aback that it wasn't in a more formal or office-like building, similar to the community centre.

Normally I'm cautious, but for some reason I ignored my doubt and decided to give it a try. I tentatively walked up the driveway, following a cardboard sign that said the entrance to the Gnostic Movement was at the back. I walked up two steps through a fly-screened door into a back sun-room adjoining an open kitchen. There were several people, some waiting, some in conversation, either leaning on the bench top or sitting around the table. The lectures were held in the lounge room and the bedrooms which were furnished with chairs and mats.

The number of people was far fewer than those who turned up at the community centre for the first lecture. Perhaps they were put off when they saw the Gnostic Study Centre was just a residential house. Considering they survived on donations, it's no wonder they could not afford a more impressive building.

My curiosity was stronger than my scepticism and I continued to study with the Gnostic Movement until I completed their four courses. The first, 'Searching Within' was about consciousness and the ego. The second was 'Astral Travel & Dreams'. The third, 'Journey to Enlightenment' was about esoteric theory including karma and the wheel of life. The fourth, 'Advanced Investigation', was working with ego through awareness and meditation techniques.

I learned ways to focus the mind through concentration, and visualisation exercises to strengthen the imagination. The practice of self awareness through 'being in the moment' was a challenge to my drifting mind. I also enjoyed their vowel mantra chanting to tone and open the chakras. I always hung out for a community spirit with other participants when we compared experiences and impressions. Some were friendly but others didn't talk much and looked overly serious. I was looking for enthusiasm and a certain aliveness, as usual expecting too much.

The courses were free but I did donate some money to the kitty, about $250 in total, over the four years I studied with them. During that time, I met a woman in her 30s who had fled Scientology after suffering the usual treatment at their hands of being ostracised and swindled out of more than $100,000. When I told her Gnosticism was free, she looked uncomfortable and didn't return after that. Perhaps she was annoyed to learn, so belatedly, that wisdom does not have to cost an arm and a leg.

I studied a deeper level of theory with the Gnostic Institute of Anthropology for about a year. The contrast between the two organisations was that the Institute teachers seemed to have little direct experience of what they taught. For that reason I repeated the four Gnostic Movement courses to reinforce the practical learning I already had.

I saw progress with my self development and had a minor out of body experience after practicing their astral travel techniques on and off, but it took too much mental discipline for me for consistent results so I didn't continue with this part. During this time, I had spiritual dreams that were mystical and instructive.

Spiritual dreams are not the same as the normal dreams which are replays of the day or churning over suppressed emotional issues. These dreams are the ones you don't forget. The fact that I started to get them after joining the Gnostic Movement does not mean they were the holy grail of truth. It's simply a response to spiritual effort no matter what the source. I was starting to feel that the power struggle (if I could call it that) between the consciousness and the ego, really is the engine room of spiritual progress.

I was always looking forward to having my mind blown away at regular intervals by the new ideas at the lectures. To me it felt exciting because I was exposed to ideas I had not come across before, fresh and raw like a new frontier. It felt adventurous to step outside the box of highly processed and packaged ideas we are spoon fed in our consumer culture and education all our lives. Yet I didn't stay with the Gnostic Movement.

The Signs that All was Not Right

It wasn't long before red flags starting popping up for me while I attended the Gnostic Study Centre once a week. There was mostly a quiet and serious atmosphere and their membership wasn't growing. It seemed to be the same people each week and few of the newcomers, who came from the introductory lecture, returned.

I could not understand why people were subdued. There were generally two others and myself who were the only ones asking questions during the lectures. To this day, I never worked out why this was the case. If a person went to all the trouble to show up, and they knew it was outside the norm, then surely they would be more curious and willing to open up.

At first I wouldn't face it square on, but I could swear there were shadows of the Catholic guilt-trip and fear in the general atmosphere at the study centre. In some ways their version of spirituality made you feel like a brick in the wall which is the last thing I wanted. They didn't mention the soul much, and spoke only in terms of the consciousness (divine spark) and the egos. To their credit, the teachers didn't pretend to have all the answers. Once I asked them about one of their ideas which didn't make sense to me and the teacher admitted he didn't know. I also asked if they meant soul when they spoke of consciousness, but received a vague and inconclusive answer. It was like they themselves were unsure.

Their definition of ego was a bit strange and old world. Common sense says everyone has a single ego with many faces but the Gnostics used the expression 'multiplicity of the egos'. They referred to ego in the plural, as in egos. This meant anger was one ego, laziness was another ego, greed was yet another ego, and so on, and that they entered a person in a moment of weakness, much like a dark force with a life of its own. This idea of ego caused a defensive approach to ego work and, in a worse case, a person could feel like a fortress facing constant ambush as if in a civil war. At this rate, a person could be forgiven for feeling outnumbered by multiple egos. This could explain the serious atmosphere at the study centre.

Like Buddhism, the Gnostics believe in the Wheel of Life (Samsara). This is the cycle of birth and death of many lives in the physical world due to karma. The Gnostic version of salvation said you need to get rid of 50 percent of your egos to get off the wheel of life and continue your growth in a higher dimension where the dominant emotion is not fear, like it is here, but love.

They said the personality and the physical body are the vehicle for the consciousness and the egos to express themselves. This meant the consciousness and the egos live on for the next incarnations. I didn't admit it then (not even to myself) but the lack of mention of the soul bothered me. This was starting to sound like the 'brick in the wall' theory of a human being - that we are no more than an undifferentiated cell of consciousness in a bigger God body.

My hope that Gnosticism was the way to truth and enlightenment went through a slow unravelling after I came upon another one of their strange ideas. This one was a doozy. They said a person reincarnates as a human only 108 times. If they didn't get rid of 50 percent of their egos by the end of their last human life, they began to devolve into the animal kingdom. I am certain this idea also fed the serious atmosphere at the study centre. How was one supposed to know if they were on their last human life? Because this mistaken belief is found nowhere else at all, in any spiritual teachings, I rejected it. Assertions like this really are an ideology of fear that is a trademark of a cult.

Unfortunately, the way the Gnostics taught how to handle the ego was creating a dead-end in spiritual growth. At first it was all heady, understanding the ego and its offshoots - how it manifests with thoughts, moods, feelings, body language, and physical effects. But their methods for working on the ego were over-complicated. Their main strength, as I saw it, was their understanding of how ego manifests in the mind, emotions and body. I've not read or come across any other explanation of that aspect that is so practical (explained in Chapter 3 – Ego Anatomy).

They said the egos had to be 'disintegrated' through a reflective meditation technique called 'dying to yourself'. All you had to do was spot an ego working in you then immediately say to yourself 'Divine Mother, disintegrate it'. According to them, it's the feminine aspect of God that has the power to overcome the ego. Yet they said the 'dying to yourself' technique only temporarily removes the ego.

The permanent way was an advanced technique that focused on one specific ego at a time during meditation. The 'meditation on an ego' was an analytical method with many steps that started with retrospection (recall the ego's origin, like a childhood memory), then inner observation (how it manifests in general), and finally, investigation (try to intuit the current trigger for the ego). The meditation concluded with the Egyptian mantra (Laaa Raaa Ssss). Whenever I tried this method on myself I found I had to break my concentration to glance at my notes to see what was the next step.

At first, I went along with it all because there is always a stage, before you admit to something being wrong, when you desperately want to believe. Yet I couldn't help feeling that I didn't have the full picture, and that feeling grew in the back of my mind. Progress with the ego, the Gnostic way, was slow and tortuous. I also discovered that trying to eliminate or disintegrate the ego, or declare war on it in any way, only reinforces it. It wasn't until I discovered other spiritual teachings, and synthesised my own methods, that I started to make real progress with my ego.

After spending six years with them, I left. I think the clincher was the 108 human life limit which I had not heard of anywhere, and none of the teachers could explain it. Here was a subtle hypocrisy at play; they taught that the truth is felt and experienced, yet were willing to hold ideas that had no common-sense basis in reality, or means to prove, let alone experience directly.

I wanted to tell you of my experience with Gnosticism because it doesn't matter what your spiritual starting point is, even if the religion, cult or spiritual group is far from perfect. If you are discerning and genuine with your intentions, you will be able to sift out the gems from the glass. Being discerning like this is not something we learn because we are conditioned to believe that if there is a mistake found in something, then the whole thing must be no good.

After I left the Gnostics to continue my research and study independently, I found teachings that spoke of the individual soul and that we incarnate to individuate. Because we have many lives, the aggregate of all our lives enriches our soul. One soul, many lives. Rather than simply *know* the difference between love and its opposite, we *understand* the difference at a much deeper and richer level, and that is through the direct experience of lack of love.

I have found that spiritual teachings that don't have religious roots, are more joyful, expansive, free and loving. So despite my experience with Gnosticism, I was not put off spirituality. Instead I became more curious than ever. I saw there is a real difference between mainstream religion and ancient spirituality. When I was treading water after leaving the Gnostics, I had a dream which advised me to find my own ground.

A Spiritual Friend

Around this time, I was looking to work more from home because of my young daughter. Since I am a technical writer, I decided to learn copywriting for the web and thought this would be an easy transition. I read a very persuasive sales letter for an online course. Normally I am not a soft sell but I took the plunge and bought the course materials. I used the online forum to communicate with other students about the course work.

It was there I met a woman called Jeni who lived in New Mexico, USA. She was a 40 year old stay-at-home mom of two boys, third-generation American from German/Norwegian ethnicity. She answered a question I posted on the forum about an assignment we had to do. We started chatting when she told me she was coming to Sydney with her husband for a short business trip.

We took our conversation offline when we started to talk about other things besides the course. After that, an email pen-friendship started. We emailed each other on and off for about a year, then one day, after a lapse in our emails, she sent me one that started:

> 'Hello my friend,
> I was just sitting down to do some writing and thought I'd start by writing to my far away friend. I got to thinking of some of the things I put in my last email and thought I may have offended you. I know that some people are very serious about their religion. I hope I didn't make you upset by saying that there are no right religions. It is just something that I have come to believe in the past 14 years of my spiritual journey.'

She explained that she no longer attended church regularly or considered herself a Catholic. She did a lot of personal research into spirituality and from that she felt she was gaining a better understanding of God. In the final paragraph of her email letter, she said:

> 'I'm sorry I'm just babbling on and on today, I don't know what my problem is. But, I was wondering if you could tell me about Gnostic Christianity and how it differs from regular Christianity. What led you to Gnosticism? I would love to hear your story. I am anxious to hear more about it and what brought you to that particular religion. Being on my own spiritual journey, I am always interested in hearing how other people's journeys have brought them to their place in life.'

I was surprised and delighted to have someone ask me about spirituality so I replied:

> 'My dear Jeni,
> I didn't reply to your last email yet because I've been so busy the last two weeks. This one is going to be long, so grab a cuppa and settle in, because you just prodded a deep sweet spot in me.....'

I told her I was not offended by her assertions about religion and that I always try to keep an open mind. I explained how I came to study with the Gnostics and why I left. I also pointed out that the timing of us meeting and opening up to each other was spooky indeed. I said:

> 'When we met I had nowhere to go, spiritually speaking. I hit a wall with the Gnostics, I discovered that I had more questions and comments than most people there. I felt alone and perplexed. I had to leave, especially after two of their best teachers left to go to England to set up a study centre there.

The remaining teachers are not exactly a lively bunch.'

Jeni was touched by my story. After that, our emails became more regular as we discussed a variety of spiritual topics and compared notes. The emails got longer and longer to the point that we started to reply in a Word document. One day when the document blew out to 60 pages, Jeni carved it up into four parts. Then each part continued with its own thread. I called it our blogosphere and felt a bit guilty that it was growing like a wild plant, but she said:

'I love our dialogue. I have no one else here to talk to about these things that mean so much to me.'

From my personal experience, I've found that people who are spiritual can become drawn to another at a subconscious level. Even so, it's a good idea to discuss spirituality if they raise the topic, and only within the bounds of the aspect they are questioning. The reason being that we all operate within our comfort zone and that includes our views on reality. I have had people express an interest then shut down on me because I probably referred to something that conflicted with a deep-seated belief they were holding.

Spirituality is very different to the norms we have grown up with and the best way to discover it is in layers, in a way that unfolds naturally for the person seeking. If you try to convince another, like raving about the benefits of spirituality, then it won't be a genuine impulse. It is not a must or a should - it is a want. You badly need that genuine impulse from inside you because without it, you will fall over the first time you run into trouble with ego.

Chapter 2: The Ego Self

Everyone has some understanding of ego. We use expressions like 'that person has a big ego' and 'ego maniac'. Or we say of a person who loses their cool, that they are 'having a meltdown' when they are so overcome with negativity, lack of courage or objectivity, that they sink into a self-absorbed state of panic.

We recognise it takes time to get to know someone, to get behind the facades we all wear to be socially acceptable. When we do, others will say of a person 'I saw another side to him'. Another variation of the observable ego is when someone has done something criminally wrong and people will say the person was a victim of their inner demons, or their dark side. Ego, at this very basic level, is the part of the psyche that holds repressed memories or denials, and hidden aspects of the personality.

With a deeper understanding of the many facets of our selves we can be less manipulated by the see-saw of ego emotions. We fall back on ego because our society and culture thinks ego is all there is to us. I once read a post on an online forum where a person asserted their ego is what makes them individual. This is a common misperception, that ego holds our identity, our individuality, our personality. This book will explain how the opposite is true, that ego robs us of our individuality and makes us all the same.

A Possible Origin of Ego

How did ego come to dominate our consciousness? On one hand, it's a survival tool that helps us cope with the challenges of physical life. On the other hand, it's that part of our psyche that's disconnected from our origin (Love) and considers itself separate from others in a competitive way. To dig deeper, let's take a spiritual perspective by using the biblical story of Adam and Eve as a metaphor. Think of it as a folk tale for how ego began in human consciousness.

As we know, Adam and Eve were cast out from the Garden of Eden after eating the forbidden fruit from the Tree of Knowledge. Before this happened, they were in a state of innocence, but after tasting the fruit they were exposed to the concept of duality – of right and wrong. This was more than just the idea of opposites, this is more damaging. It's about Good and Evil, of something being worthy of love and something being unworthy of love, of punishment and reward, of caring and not caring.

When Adam and Eve lost their innocence, they may have felt it as a profound attack of insecurity. Even though they used their free will to make a choice, they became unsettled by a new and uncomfortable feeling, and that was doubt. This led to judgemental thinking to explain why they no longer felt certainty. They would have concluded, for the first time, that

God would not be happy with what they had done. They even speculated that God might abandon them. The prospect of rejection gave rise to the next ego layer, that of defensiveness. This caused a narrowing of understanding. The sense of unease grew and people repressed this unpleasant feeling into deeper depths of their being, never to see the light of day. This created denial, duplicity, and falseness as the next ego shrouds. The Id was created, a segregated part of the psyche that became the dumping ground for feelings that could not be faced, let alone explained, because they were too painful.

Not understanding the uneasiness, and scared of finding out why, it made sense to externalise everything. People came to think that God had an enemy and that this enemy was an equal adversary. It was easier to point a finger at something outside the self and label it bad. Casting blame on others become the most common fear avoidance tactic.

More ego layers settled like shrouds over the real self. Eventually these layers became so dense that people lost all sight of their true selves and forgot their true nature. Feeling an identity crisis, they became indignant. Pride took over and set about steering motives and actions in a way that created a separation between self and others. There was a desire to be special and apart from others. Others got hurt and retaliated. Those on the receiving end didn't try to understand the cause of the retaliation, and labelled the other person bad. They too retaliated and it started the endless tit-for-tat we all know today.

We could have continued on the path of Universal Love, but instead, we went down the road of its manufactured opposite -

the idea that there is something that does not deserve love. So, in our minds, love was withdrawn. In that case, we did not have to know ourselves or understand our deeper emotions, that seemed pointless, even too late, plus we feared what we would find.

Scape-goats were created, and like pass-the-parcel, the truth was avoided. People could not face the truth anyway because by now they no longer recognised it. Offering animal and human sacrifices were an attempt to appease a so-called angry God. Creating enemies to fight in conflicts and wars let people cast themselves as being the good one and having the God-given right to seek justice. The machine of war became an entrenched part of our civilisation and our psyche. Eventually we lost our intimacy with God until He became a warm but archaic and fuzzy concept.

Yet ego can't do away with God completely, since religion still survives today. Millions of people still hold faith, we have the Bible and miracles have been documented. Prophets have come and gone and left their legacy. So ego resorts to seeing God as a sentiment. It points a finger at the pain and suffering in the world (which ego created), and declares that if there was a universal God then why does he *allow* all these terrible things to happen in the world. This fits the typical ego way of blaming others and avoiding responsibility.

The robotic ego behaviour was so entrenched that it created deeper insecurities and lack of trust which led to negative experiences. Many people would fall into a victim mentality as they let fear convince them they were powerless. Since we lost sight of the truth, our only connection with God was through religion. Yet this is a change from a knowing in the heart, to a belief system that depended on followers having blind faith.

For that we won the grand prize by becoming utterly dependant upon authority and punitive laws. This resulted in a legal system that perpetuates the idea of victim-hood and 'senseless crime' which implies that it's pointless to try to understand causes or find the trigger. Common sense and intuition were systematically undervalued. So much so, that only experts, who are trained in a specific way, are taken seriously as having a point of view that is worth considering.

What was really strange was people's willingness to adopt convoluted, and often incoherent laws, as a substitute for common sense. It's no wonder that this led to the assumption that justice was too complicated for the average person and should be taken out of their hands to be interpreted by experts. It reminds me of that quote by Douglas Bader, World War II Royal Air Force Ace fighter, who said:

> 'Rules are for the interpretation of wise men and for the blind obedience of fools.'

Ego is heavily reinforced and fed by our culture which places enormous value on fame and material wealth, which really are attempts to be separate from others. This creates more alienation as not everyone is motivated to get rich by any means. Since there is no alternative ideal that is given as much credibility, we have learned to put a lid on any part of ourselves that doesn't conform to it.

Ego's fear of rejection is so great that our sense of self worth is usually contingent on how well we conform. The only way ego can pretend to be individual is by acquiring objects to show off and winning in competition. Ego is driven to neurosis by the pressure to conform yet straining to be special. When we used our free will to separate from God, our ego grew to fill the gap and fooled us into believing that it is real and that God is unreal.

The Evolution of Ego/Soul Research

In the early 20th century, ego was thought to be nothing more than a psychological concept. Sigmund Freud was one of the first to develop a model of the human personality. He stated that each person has three parts to their ego make-up: the Id, which is primeval, childish, impulsive, and is the self-absorbed ego. The Super Ego being the judgmental self-correcting, , and moralising part. The mediator Ego, he considered to be more conscious and mediates between the first two ego layers.

According to Freud's model, the ego triad operates in a person in the following way. A person's Ego can be aware that their Id just acted impulsively, so the Super Ego will criticise them. The Id is always in a tug-of-war with the controlling Super Ego. The mediator Ego then decides which one will win out – will the person go with their impulse then feel guilty later? Or, will they not give into their impulse, then later resent that they missed out?

One of Freud's students developed the personality theory even further between 1912 and 1917.

Carl Jung was a psychiatrist and the founder of analytical psychology. He proposed two centres of the personality – the Ego and the Self. The ego is the awake consciousness when we are not sleeping, and the Self is the total personality that includes the consciousness, the unconscious, and the ego. Jung said that while ego sees itself as separate and only, the Self is fully aware of its wholeness.[5]

When first proposed, Jung's theory of personality was criticised as being unscientific due to his lack of empirical research. He derived his conclusions from his observations and analysis as a psychiatrist; and introspection of his own thoughts, feelings and dreams. He also listened to the thoughts, feelings and dreams of his patients which helped shape his theory. Once again, testing and measuring seemed to hold more credibility than observation and experience.

The unconscious part of Self consists of two parts. The 'personal unconscious' is the store of personal experiences unique to each individual. It holds a person's memories, impressions and biases that can come into consciousness through recall. It also contains the skills we learn so well that we do them automatically (subconscious). The other part of the Self is the 'collective unconscious'. It has all the knowledge and experiences we share as a species and is the store house of universal symbols and personality archetypes. Jung also referred to it as the super-conscious.

Archetypes are models of people's behaviour and personality traits that have evolved over time from collective experience. Jung believed these archetypes exist in the collective unconscious to organize and make sense of our experiences. Jung identified four major archetypes common to all humanity. He believed them to be innate, universal and hereditary.

Jung's Four Main Archetypes

The Persona

The word 'persona' comes from the Latin word meaning mask. It's all the social masks we wear. Even though personas are not our true self, they are part of the conscious mind. Many people identify too much with a persona and think it's their whole self. Jung saw the persona as a single ego with many faces, and that we swap them around as the need dictates. If you ask a doctor what he or she does for a living, they won't say, 'I practise medicine' but rather, 'I'm a doctor'.

The Shadow

The shadow is the part of the personal unconscious and contains the parts of our selves we have disowned and buried. It ranges from suppressed memories that may be traumatic, to character traits we cut off from our conscious awareness through denial because we don't like them. These traits are usually those that don't conform to society's dictates, or were rejected by those closest to us. It is quite murky because this is where, over time, we have dumped the things we can't bring out into the open. It contains un-expressed ideas and desires, sexual impulses and hunger, antipathy towards others, and irrational fears.

Even though the shadow is present in all people, some deny this aspect of their psyche and instead project the undesirable qualities onto others. This is very common. Jung suggested that the shadow can appear in dreams or visions and may take a variety of forms. It might appear as a snake, a monster, a demon, a dragon, or some other dark, wild or exotic figure.

The Anima/Animus

The Anima is the female soul image of a man, the Animus the male soul image of a woman. The anima/animus is the true Self representing the balance of the two gender aspects within a person. It stands for the completion, unification and wholeness of the soul. In our society until very recently, the Animus soul image dominated as evidenced by the idea that rational reasoning is superior to emotions and intuition, and that intellect rules over innate intelligence. Jung believed that if one allows more balance between the Anima/Animus, he or she can bridge the gap between the unconscious and the conscious.

The Self

The Self is the unified conscious and unconscious. The creation of the Self occurs through a process known as individuation. At first, the feminine and masculine aspects are polarised, then later in the soul's development, they are balanced. We can see this in our culture. Up until the end of the 1970s, male and female roles and stereotypes were polarised. Jung often represented the Self as a circle, a square or a mandala. The Self is the whole of the psyche and contains all the other archetypes. This is extremely difficult for the conscious ego to accept.

One of the few spiritual authors or teachers who have tried to clearly define the ego (in a spiritual sense) is Dr Susan Shumsky, a spiritual teacher and author of several books, most notably the one called *Divine Revelation*. She says of the ego:

> 'The façade mind is your ego with which you identify yourself, composed of encrusted thought-forms and habit patterns. The façade body is an armour or mask that identifies you in limited ways. It's your protective shield you face the world with.

Your ego and self-image consist of many of these masks.'[6]

The ego creates what she refers to as a façade body around our true divine body. This creates the illusion of separation between us and our divine higher selves (soul). In reality, there is no division. Notice what characterises a lot of human dynamics, we doubt others very easily and it's hard to trust. Jumping to conclusions and being judgemental are rife, and all are workings of the ego. This is the mechanism that divides and conquers people all throughout time. It causes everything from coldness and indifference to oppression and war. No one opens up to the other and this became an unconscious default that is deeply entrenched in our culture.

Discovering the Super-conscious

During the 1980s, the super-conscious was explored by Dr Michael Newton through his hypnotic regression therapy. He has a doctorate in Counselling Psychology, is a certified Master Hypnotherapist, and a member of the American Counselling Association. It is worth noting that since 1958, the American Medical Association accepted hypnosis as a valid medical tool.

Newton's discovery of the super-conscious was by accident. He originally used his regression therapy to access patients' early childhood memories as a treatment for psychological disorders. When he was asked by some patients if he would do past life regression, he refused because he came from a traditional academic background and thought the concept of past lives was unorthodox.

Years later, a patient came to him about a pain in his side that could not be explained by medical doctors. They had concluded it was psychosomatic and advised the patient it would probably go away if he stopped focusing on it. Dr Newton did his standard regression to the patient's childhood, but found nothing. While the patient was still in a deep hypnotic state, Dr Newton asked him to go to the origin of the pain. The patient started to describe a scene at the Battle of Somme in World War I.

Dr Newton was immediately sceptical, so he quizzed the patient what army division was he in, who was he fighting, and what uniform badge did he wear on his arm. The patient answered each question, and since Dr Newton is an amateur war historian, he recognised the patient's answers as correct. From this he realised past lives could be real, but continued to research to validate his finding.

A second patient came along and Dr Newton did the same steps, first regressing to childhood, found nothing, then asked her to go to the source of her pain. This particular patient went into a deep hypnosis quite readily, and it was with this patient that he accessed the super-conscious. He made the remarkable discovery that as souls, we seem to have a life between earth lives - meaning our earth lives are more like excursions away from home.

Over many years, through trial and error, he pioneered his Life Between Lives regression therapy where he accesses the super-conscious of his patients under hypnosis. He says in his book, *Journey of Souls*:

'Patients in a super-conscious state are not
particularly motivated to volunteer information
about the whole plan of soul life in the spirit world.
One must have the right set of keys for specific
doors.'[7]

He continued to access the super-conscious of this patients
because it proved to be far more effective for their healing.
What dissolved his scepticism was the consistency of his
patients' reports while in that state. It didn't matter if they
were deeply religious or atheist, or what ethnicity they were.
They, in his words:

'...all displayed a remarkable consistency in
responding to questions about the spirit world.
People even used the same words and graphic
descriptions...when discussing their lives as souls.'

How is it possible to reach the soul through hypnosis?
According to Dr Newton, imagine the mind is like three
concentric circles, each smaller than the last and embedded in
the other. The first outer layer is the conscious mind, the
second layer is the subconscious which is accessed through
hypnosis to uncover childhood or past life memories. The third
circle, at the core, is what he refers to as the super-conscious
mind. This is our real identity, concealed by the subconscious
and all the ego layers. The super-conscious may be the soul
itself.

Now that past life regression therapy has gained increasing
acceptance, we can see that from each life (or incarnation) our
soul accumulates strengths and weaknesses. Our soul, our
immortal self, will seek to transform the weaknesses into

strengths through the next incarnation that best expresses the aspects that need working on. This is where the ego is indispensable, but we forget what we are here for, and most of us become subjugated by the ego and live under its spell all our lives. You could say that such a life is wasted, but the Universe is infinitely patient and you always get another chance. Through the experiences of life, and the upbringing and cultural backdrop, a person can expose their ego weaknesses, find their strengths, and figure out ways to improve themselves in the process. Since fear is the common denominator of ego, you could say the purpose of our life is to learn how to become fearless, or at least, less fearful.

The Strange Gnostic Multiple Ego

There is a mirror difference between the psychological model of ego by Freud and Jung, and the spiritual model by 20th century Gnosticism. Where Jung identified ego as being in the conscious part of the mind, the Gnostic idea is that when ego dominates the conscious mind, the person is unaware and is spiritually unconscious. Freud defined our psyche in terms of three ego selves: the super ego, ego and id; and like the Gnostics, did not seem to recognise the soul.

Gnostic thinking says that without this knowing of the true self (the divine essence or consciousness), unpleasant situations or feelings just seem to happen to a person. If a person is offended or feeling depressed, they succumb to these feelings even though they are not beneficial. A person in this state is like a puppet on a string, their state of mind totally depends on outer circumstances and how people are treating them. If feelings like unexplained sadness rise up from within, the person looks for a quick fix and falls into a pleasure/pain cycle which entrenches them in the ego state.

According to modern Gnosticism, their theory of the psyche consists of three main parts:

The Sub-conscious (ego)

The personal sub-conscious (not to be confused with subconscious) was defined as the drives, desires, emotions, instincts and impulses that are the self-centred states of ego which originate from the animal kingdom. When you observe a more intelligent animal, like a mammal, they have similar reactions and instincts that humans have but ours are more complex. We have developed the intellect which has a greater capacity for evil. The sub-conscious is seen as the source of inner darkness and the cause of all suffering. When we are lost in a thought, or a daydream, we are in the sub-consciousness of ego and spiritual consciousness is dormant.

The Gnostic expression 'multiplicity of the egos' instead of the singular ego, is puzzling because it makes more sense to see a single ego with many faces, like Jung's Persona archetype and Shumsky's facade. For some reason the Gnostics subscribe to the idea that the ego faces, like anger, pride, greed, and vanity, are separate egos. This means anger is one ego, lust is another ego, and so on. It is described this way in the Gnostic Movement's textbook *The Peace of the Spirit Within*:

> 'The different egos reside in the fifth dimension, each one is a completely separate entity. They

enter and leave the person according to the opportunity being available to them and they take their food from the person's psychic energy. They enter the person one at a time, ... When one leaves another ego comes in, it can then override or contradict previous ones.'[8]

So the Gnostics see the ego as a multiple set of entities outside a person that manipulate them like a robot in the same way nature's program keeps animals within certain bounds of behaviour for their function and survival. According to Gnosis, these ego states are called selves, or I's, or 'psychological adjuncts with all of them having the continuity of the feeling of 'I' or 'me' in common'. Each human has the capacity to remove them and to replace them with a different array of being like perception, intelligence, compassion, wisdom and love.

The Personality

In Gnostic theory, the personality of a life is formed by the age of seven, and is determined by ethnicity, parents, education, temperament and upbringing. The personality forms a grid for the expression of the egos and consciousness. It also contains attributes of our identity like the skills we acquire and personal tastes. Different personalities have different egos that dominate. In their textbook it says:

'When it's said that a person has pride, it's not the personality that is proud, but that the personality is a vehicle for the ego of pride to express itself, through mannerisms or words.'

The Gnostic theory of ego sounds like it's drawn from the Catholic Seven Deadly sins, which are archetype (or root) egos, and could be why the Gnostics chose to externalise the ego. I'll discuss the Catholic concept in more detail in Chapter 3 - Ego Anatomy.

The Consciousness

This is the divine essence of a person, the spark of God. All spiritual growth, wisdom, intelligence, intuition, love, peace, psychic abilities, and mystical experiences take place here. By tapping into the consciousness, the muddiness of the egos can be avoided. The way to do this is by 'being in the now' (in the Buddhist sense). This means being alert to when your mind drifts into the past, or ruminates about the future, and consciously shifting attention back to the present moment. The more often you can do this throughout the day, the more conscious you become. This is why self-awareness is considered a vital skill. When the consciousness is sufficiently developed, the mind can be its tool.

In retrospect, I couldn't get over the Gnostic lack of mention of the soul. Is this because the soul is attributed to an individual? This overlooking of the personal soul and its individuation is what started to challenge my faith in the Gnostics. How could we ever have built a society, an industry, a nation, if it were not for the very individual drives and diverse abilities, skills, talents, motivations and qualities of the variety of people that make up a whole civilisation? It is only through patience, diligence, sacrifice and cooperation that anything lasting was built. These are not self-centred ego qualities.

The other difficulty I had with the Gnostic theory was that to externalise the ego into a multiple was disempowering. The idea of 'dying to yourself' and eliminating the ego would threaten ego's sense of survival. It turns the whole spiritual effort into a defensive battle rather than a process of reclamation. For this reason, Gnostic theory helped me understand my psychological make up yet I was still a swirling soup of conflicting emotions.

New Age Understanding of Ego

As I learned and researched more about current thinking on the human psyche, the Gnostic multiple ego made less sense to me. It seemed to deny the individual soul and I started to see it as arcane and based on an old-world (pre-psychology) definition that was falling back on medieval dark forces. On one hand, it implies that we live under siege, on the positive side, it implies that we can be (or our true nature is) pure. I believe their intention was that a person could work on their mental and emotional states to become less hospitable to the 'egos'.

The Catholics were the first to externalise the ego with their Seven Deadly Sins concept, but suggest only guilt and repentance. This is like the man who keeps feeding the beggar one fish a day but never teaching him how to fish. The Gnostics try to address the challenge in a practical sense but I can't find a justification that an ego is a separate entity and is outside a person. If I experience anger, the emotion is mine and I should take responsibility for it.

It's true that negative emotions drain your energy, but to say the ego of anger enters a person in a moment of weakness, sounds like they are ambushed from outside. When the Gnostics speak of 'death to the ego' and 'dying to yourself', the conscious ego seems to cooperate but the unconscious ego, the shadow side, is left holding the baton and sees a threat. It is like declaring war on yourself and you can't get away with that. Ego will resist.

Another understanding of ego is that it's a by-product of the misuse of our free will. Other spiritual teachers and authors have observed that ego should not be eliminated. Adrian Cooper, author of *Our Ultimate Reality*, writes:

> 'The Ego is not something that can be destroyed or transcended because it is a vital aspect of who we are. The ultimate objective is not to attempt to destroy the Ego but rather to subjugate the ego, bringing it under control.'9

To reassure ego so it can't block your spiritual growth, it's a good idea to see its constructive potential. Take the ego face of pride, it can create drive and ambition in a person that leads to achievement. For example, someone may be determined to be the best at something because their pride will not allow them to identify and remain in their current situation, like coming from a poor background. They may feel a sense of shame as they've seen their parents struggle all their lives and get nowhere. Their pride decides they want something better. They become driven because they have nothing to fall back on (insecurity), and this is the spur to never give up. This could be an athlete who qualifies for the Olympics. On the surface it may appear as raw ambition, but in the process they inspire others to extend themselves beyond their perceived limits.

The ego faces of anger and stubbornness can also have a constructive aspect. Take the times when we stand up for what we believe. Even though ideas about social injustice and how it can be addressed will tend to come from the soul, it can be the ego traits of stubbornness and always being right, that make a person like a dog with a bone and drives them to push for reform. When we stand up against oppression of others, environmental degradation, animal cruelty, and manage to convince those with a means to make a difference, and they do, then that is an example of when ego and soul work together to change the world for the better.

Ego also lets us operate within the limits of space and time in the third dimension. Like the brain organ, the ego is a constrictor because it localizes our awareness in a linear fashion. This means we are always moving forward in a line away from the past and towards the future. In our bubble of the present, we can focus on sequence and detail and this lets us create things in the physical world. By contrast, Spirit and the soul live a timeless infinite existence.

According to new age spirituality, God desired to express and observe beyond a pure energy state. To achieve this, sparks of the divine took physical form. If we are like the shards of God (but individuated), then our soul came into a physical body for a focused experience to express itself as one unique aspect of God. The best way to do this is to engage in relationship with other souls and co-create with them. It's not that we are fighting evil, we are fighting the illusion of evil that we created with our ego mind. In a big picture sense, we came here to lose our way then find it again.

The following quote from Sri Aurobindo, the early 20th century scholar, philosopher, revolutionary, and yogi, captures this and is an excellent example of what I mean by non-religious spiritual sources being the most joyful, loving and free. He says:

> 'What you ask, was the beginning of it all?
> And it is this...
> Existence that multiplied itself for sheer delight of being
> And plunged into numberless trillions of forms
> So that It might find Itself innumerably.'

Another spiritual teacher I admire, Jerry Hirschfield, started out as an electrical engineer in the aerospace industry. After losing his job during the recession of the 1970s, he went through a period of adjustment and, while reassessing his life, he battled severe depression.

After a spiritual awakening, he wrote his first book *Twelve Steps for Everyone* for people having emotional or life crisis problems. He went back to university to study counselling and psychology and practiced as a marriage and family therapist in California. He spoke of the role of ego in his book *My Ego, My Higher Power and I*, and has an insightful and sensitive appreciation of the ego's place in the scheme of things:

> 'Your True Self is an Everlasting, Eternal, Spiritual Being made of Pure Love Energy. We are not in

close contact with our True Self because we have allowed It to be overshadowed by our ego, with which we are almost completely identified. Our ego is the part of our Soul which we created, and which does not want to follow the divine guidance within us. Therefore, it is the seat of our perceived imperfections. As a result of our identification with our egos, we feel separate, alone, and afraid.'[10]

What is our true nature then? You could say that state of openness and love that existed before the so-called Original Sin. It was a *knowing* of God's existence, as opposed to having to believe or have faith, and a clear sense of purpose in the scheme of things. It was about being potent and fearless. There was a unity with others and with nature.

So leaving the Gnostics to find my own ground, was a positive development since there were plenty of constructive sources of spiritual wisdom. I had the freedom to explore the truth myself but also the responsibility of having to be discerning and to make the best sense of it to apply it usefully.

My spiritual friend Jeni's calling to find her own ground came to her before we met. She admitted her reaction had been the opposite to mine. This was understandable as her context was different from mine. She had made the conscious decision to leave her Catholic faith that she grew up with. It wasn't as easy a choice for her to follow through, as her family were more religious than mine. She said:

'For me, I was breaking free of organized religion, breaking free of everyone believes the same thing. I was scared out of my mind. I felt completely lost. The thought of breaking away, being an individual, and doing my own thing TERRIFIED me. It was only after our friendship began, did I realize how wonderful and beautiful being an individual and doing your own thing could be. It was completely freeing and a wonderful, beautiful feeling.'

Jeni had looked into some of the Gnostic teachings after I told her of my experiences. Even though she didn't delve into it as deeply as I did, we discussed many of their ideas about ego and consciousness. I was relieved because now I felt confident I could rely on myself to explore the Truth without an intermediary like religion, and for that I felt liberated.

Chapter 3: Ego Anatomy

The ego of a person has many faces, but at the core of ego is Fear. When I refer to an ego like anger, I mean the ego face of anger not the Gnostic multiple egos. Coming to the realisation that ego is the same in all of us was greatly helped by the dialogue I was having with Jeni. We confided to each other about issues with our family and other life challenges. We discussed how we were handling our relationships, and while working on our ego, we started to see positive results. I helped Jeni with an emotional issue involving her sister and she encouraged me to open up to her about stress I was dealing with at work. I said to her in one of my emails:

> 'Thanks for hearing my vent, and your tips and advice. In fact it feels like I've come full circle in a way. At one point I was giving you similar advice to what you are giving me today. So I'll try to stop handicapping myself and just live in the moment and take one step at a time. I am so glad to have you for a friend that I can show myself to you as I really am.'

There were times when we took a step back and marvelled at how similar our ways of thinking were and wondered if we were talking to each other as ego personalities or as souls.

Jeni said:

> 'There you go again! It's that spooky thing where I feel like you're actually in my head and can read my thoughts. This is almost precisely how it goes with me.'

I replied:

> 'It's not that. I've learned that thought processes using the ego mind are much the same in all people. But yes, I do think we are a lot alike. I've never been able to even come close to the subjects that we talk about with anyone else.'

Even though I have a more academic background than Jeni, I didn't assume I knew more than her because it's all about direct experience. I wanted to learn from her as much as she was learning from me. The intellect segregates people, but intelligence when communicated the way we did, is universal and unifying. Much of our dialogue was heart-felt and soul to soul:

I said:

> 'We should share our struggles because chances are we are struggling with the same thing at the same time. Honestly, life sometimes feels like a snakes & ladders board game.'

Jeni replied:

'I believe we do share our struggles already, don't we? That's what my SJ [spiritual journey] has felt like, Snakes and Ladders. Great description.'

I said:

'Through you I have learned that we are all made of the same stuff, have the same hopes, dreams and failings. Through you I have learned not to judge people and many truths have sunk in sooner because of our dialogue.'

Jeni replied:

'That is very sweet. Yes, many things have sunk in for me also because of our blogs.'

Ego was a topic we discussed among other spiritual topics, but it was more of a practical focus as we applied our shared understanding to improve our emotional life. Jeni had more experience with tapping into the higher self and I was more versed with ego. I would help her with ego issues while she would give me insights into how to hear the 'small still voice' more often.

When we discussed the Catholic Seven Deadly Sins concept, I told her about the Gnostic idea of the 'five inferior centres in the body' where the ego can be felt. Combining these two theories made the ego more visible to us and it became obvious there is a stark difference between soul and ego. Let's look at both theories in turn.

The Seven Deadly Sins with Conquering Virtues

The Catholic Church regards sin as coming from seven major root egos which they call the Seven Deadly Sins. These are the cardinal sins which are serious enough to send you to purgatory (the no-man's land between earth and hell).

This takes a crime and punishment view of wrong-doing, and it's a shame because it assumes that people sin because they are bad or tempted for no reason. These seven deadly sins are contrasted with their opposite virtues. This is a clue that if you stop indulging in one of these egos, the energy you forgo in expressing the vice can be used towards cultivating the virtue.

The Seven Deadly Sins concept does not appear in the Bible as such but it can be traced back to the 4th century A.D. when a Christian monk named Ponticus made up his own sin list based on the behaviours he observed in the people of his day. His list was the following: gluttony, fornication/prostitution, greed, pride, sadness (self-absorption), wrath (anger), boasting (pride), and dejection (depression).

The early Church adopted the concept and the list was translated from Greek into Latin and used for educational and devotional purposes. In 590 AD, Pope Gregory I revised the list to be: lust, gluttony, greed, sloth, wrath, envy, and pride. The list was cemented into Roman Catholic tradition for centuries to come after the Italian poet Dante Alighieri (1265-1321) used them in his epic tale *The Divine Comedy*.

Here are the Catholic Seven Deadly Sins and their corresponding virtues. These root egos have been around since the beginning of time. The Gnostics call them the 'causal egos'. It is interesting that Fear is not mentioned.

Ego Vice	Corresponding Virtue
Pride	Humility / Modesty
Envy	Kindness / Charity
Lust	Love / chastity
Anger	Patience / tolerance
Gluttony	Moderation
Greed/Avarice	Generosity
Sloth/Apathy	Diligence [11]

These are the ego archetypes from which all the smaller personal egos are derived. Take Pride, it has many tentacles like vanity, stubbornness, and arrogance. With vanity, its opposite would be modesty. There's a difference between taking a compliment graciously and revelling in it. The opposite of arrogance could be humility. The virtue of humility is a type of letting go because you release all pretense and feel gratitude for the things you have, however small they may be. Humility is a powerful virtue and is closely aligned with Love.

On average, we have up to three of the ego vices that dominate our personality. For me it's Pride and Anger while others appear in smaller ways, and there's one that makes a guest appearance now and then. When a particular ego is observed, it can be managed. By spending conscious time reflecting on its opposite virtue, you become less hospitable to the ego.

In the book *The Masters and Their Retreats* by Mark Prophet and Elizabeth Clare Prophet, they say that everyone has three major recurring tests in their lives. Clare Prophet says the following from a channelled message:

> 'Most people on earth have three knots in consciousness that hold them back, pull them back. These knots are so obvious, right beneath their noses, that they fail to see them year after year. Some pass from the screen of life in the change called death never having realized that they missed the most obvious - the most obvious of matters that they came into embodiment to correct.'[12]

It sounds like a blueprint for effective living that we have 'three points of acceleration and attainment' to work on, and three self-limiting points to eliminate.

Here are two quizzes you can do:

Getting to Know Yourself Questions:

1. What are your three strongest personality traits where you show the greatest strength of character and where you are consistent no matter what?

2. What are three negative qualities, those traits that hold you back or prevent you from experiencing a sense of wholeness and inner peace?

3. What would be the opposite of each of those negative qualities?

Matching Vices and Virtues

1. Using the Catholic sins list, take three of the vices that you believe you have and write them down in one column.

2. In the second column, write what you believe would be the corresponding virtue of each vice.

3. Now consider each vice, say anger, and recall the last time you became angry. Be sure to recall it mentally not emotionally. If you find emotion creeping in, stop.

4. Now think of a quality (more than one if you can) which is the opposite of this vice. If you are not sure, think about what kind of emotion the vice gave you last time you experienced it, and match it with the opposite emotion.

5. Name that opposite emotion. The next time you feel the emotion of anger, you can recall the opposite and positive emotion you named.

Regarding point 5., you can be quite specific as a generic approach may not deal with your situation. For example, say the last time you got angry you didn't lash out but you felt tense inside. So in that instance, the opposite emotion could be compassion – like finding a reason to feel sorry for the person instead of angry. But if you did lash out, then the opposite virtue in that instance could be tolerance and forgiveness.

The Five Inferior Centres (a Gnostic treatment)

I came to understand ego in a deeper sense when I learned the Gnostic concept of the Five Inferior Centres in the body where ego manifests as emotional and physical sensations. The origin of this concept is unclear but it may have come from the early 20th century Gnostic master, Samael Aun Weor.[13]

Part of the development of self awareness is to understand how ego feels. According to modern Gnosticism, the ego manifests from one of these centres or a combination, and they can flow from one centre to the other. The centres also correspond with five of the main seven chakra points.

It's almost like we are living with something magical – through our choices these chakras points can provide us with strength, love and energy, or, the flipside, doubt, fear and illness. This is important to know because ego work is not just a mental exercise but one that involves the whole being. You can identify the physical sensations from an ego emotion as well as its feedback loop between thoughts and feelings.

The Gnostic Five Inferior Centres [14]

The Intellectual Centre:

The intellect is master of the rational mind and is responsible for thought processes and reasoning. This centre, when over-used, produces the symptoms of over-thinking and the chatter box mind. It likes to be right and will go to great lengths to justify and rationalise its position.

It likes to complicate things that may be straight-forward, preferring over-specialised expertise and reductionism instead of common sense objectivity, directness and simplicity. This can lead to blind-spots in problem solving.

When the intellect runs riot, it starts to operate in terms of exclusivity, like creating jargon in bodies of knowledge when there are normal dictionary words that would suffice. There is a joke that epitomises this:

> A man sees his doctor because he feels he has no energy all the time. The doctor examines him and finds nothing wrong, so he comes to the conclusion, and tells the man, that he is just plain lazy. The man asks the doctor, 'Can you give me the medical term so I can tell my wife?

The flip-side virtue of this inferior centre, is that reductionism has allowed a deeper understanding of the material world that has led to scientific and medical discoveries, inventions, and improvement in the material quality of life. It allows us to plan with detail and accuracy and build structures. While this centre contains all the tools and abilities of the mind, it lacks heart.

The Emotional Centre:

The emotional centre is located in the solar plexus area from the navel to the heart and in the grand sympathetic nervous system. Emotions are very powerful and can overwhelm the intellect because thoughts come and go but emotions last much longer.

If someone hurts your feelings, you may feel it in the stomach, almost like you were punched in the gut. It also manifests in the chest – this is when people refer to heartache. The emotion of fear, in this centre, feels like butterflies in the stomach, and a gut ache, or an ache in the chest.

Emotions release chemicals in the body which affect us positively or negatively. When a person is very emotional it becomes hard to think clearly. The intellect and emotional centres very often feed off each other. This centre, coupled with the intellect, can produce strong feelings of fear, upset or anger that are hard to let go.

The flipside virtue of the emotional centre is that when experiencing positive emotions like love and compassion and a sense of fun, it creates joy, nourishes relationships, and spreads peace and harmony among people.

The Sexual Centre:

This centre is located in the genital organs and holds the power of creation and reproduction. This centre has the highest frequency and will rob the other centres of energy if it becomes unbalanced, according to the Gnostics.

As with the intellect, this centre can enslave or free us. The hunger for love is so deeply rooted in us, that the shadow side of love which is lust, arises out of lack of love or inability to express love, and becomes a vulgar, objectified and grabbing instant gratification. When crimes of passion occur it's because this centre, being the most powerful, can unbalance a person's intellectual and emotional state to such an extent that they are driven to near insanity. The flipside virtue of this centre is love-based erotic sexuality and healthy vitality.

The Motor Centre:

The motor centre is located in the upper part of the dorsal spine. It takes care of the sublimated activities of movement, like the autonomic functions of walking, driving, and any other activity we become proficient enough to do subconsciously.

Our emotional state affects our bodily movements. We can tell when someone is tense by they way they move their body. With the emotion of anger, body movements become jerky, hands shake, the face scowls and the voice changes tone. It shows in nervous habits like shaking a leg while sitting, finger tapping, or a twitch in the facial muscles.

The flipside of this centre is that with positive emotions, it makes a person energetic, physically coordinated, light on their feet, and more graceful in their physical movements.

The Instinctive Centre:

This centre is located in the lower part of the dorsal spine and takes care of impulses and functions that are not conscious, like digestion and survival instinct.

It's the primitive centre that holds the fight or flight response. It can cause people to freak out when a situation calls for clear headed thinking. It manifests as sudden physical or verbal abuse, or, running away in panic from a scene of an accident. If someone startles you then your body jumps and you may in a flash assume a stance of self defence.

The flipside of this centre is that in prehistoric days, instinct kept humans alert to danger. In those days it paid to be suspicious and physically on guard. Today, it is instinct that causes you to turn around when someone is staring at you. If you trip, your hands automatically come forward to break your fall.

Even though the Gnostic Five Inferior Centres is based on the concept of multiple egos entering a person, it is still a useful concept if, instead of considering them as ego entry points, they are like an early warning system of ego rising. It provides a physical and emotional framework for self-observation and self-awareness. Without this awareness, a person's understanding of ego remains at an intellectual level.

Reconciling Ideas on Ego

Logic and experience show that the ego is a single entity in a person that wears many masks as described by Jung's Persona archetype and Shumsky's facades. Freud originally defined the basic and generic ego types we all have. The Id is the lowest and most primitive emotional part that is fear, anger and hostility, and the shadow. The Mediator Ego is the wardrobe of facades we wear all day and the contradictory personality traits we all have. The Super Ego would be the authoritarian, the one that judges the worth of everything, the inner critic, and the control freak.

A spiritual understanding of ego, as an overlay to the psychological understanding, is the most holistic and workable model of ego in the context of the soul. To simplify it further, imagine that your consciousness is composed of a Higher self and a Lower Self. This idea is present in many non-religious spiritual texts like Susan Shumsky's teachings and those of the late Elizabeth Clare Prophet, and many others.

The Higher self is our immortal part, our Soul, as defined by Jung as the Self. The Lower Self is the less conscious and more primitive part, the ego, which was defined by Freud. If there wasn't this dual nature within us, then our psyche would be flatter, both in our waking and sleeping states. We would not encounter irrational fears that go against our self-interest or experience self-sabotage. We would not have contradictory personality traits like when we force our interest because the ego says so, only to find at the last minute that a part of us withdraws.

We would be able to switch off our thoughts at will, indefinitely. Random acts of kindness would not give people heart-felt satisfaction, and would not occur if there was nothing to be gained. Fine art and music have no reason for being. We don't need them for survival or productivity. As for love, you only need a mating instinct to propagate the species and a maternal instinct to protect and nurture offspring.

Using the concept of a higher self and a lower self may seem like another duality but it's the simplest and most direct way of distinguishing ego from soul. If you like turning ideas over in your mind, there is a way to reconcile spiritual ideas if you don't have a spiritual friend to compare notes.

A useful reasoning method was devised by the early 19th century German philosopher, Georg Hegel. He wondered about the nature of reality, a lot, and knew that the mind likes to make comparisons and draw conclusions. This means that every argument has a counter-argument, every point of view has an opposite view. When we look at one and then the other, we then draw a distinction or a conclusion between the two.

Hegel formed a dialectic reasoning process called 'Thesis, Antithesis, Synthesis'[15]. Here is how it works: a thesis is a single idea; the antithesis is the opposite of that idea. The synthesis comes about by reconciling the two opposing ideas. The synthesis can become a new thesis, which naturally has its antithesis, and the process begins again until truth is discovered. To demonstrate how this works, let's use the example of a drinking glass containing some water:

THESIS: Your idea is that the glass is half-full of water.

ANTITHESIS: You realise you only took into account the volume of water in the glass and not the empty space inside as well. Your counter to the first idea is that the glass is actually half-empty.

SYNTHESIS: Now you reason that the whole space inside the glass is occupied by water and air. So yes, the glass is still half full, but if you were thirsty and you looked at the glass, you would see it as half empty.

Hegel's approach is very handy if you want to zoom in on an idea, and then out again for a broader view. It will help to tell the difference between a subjective point of view and an objective one. When I started to read other spiritual sources, I found ideas that agreed with the Gnostic teachings and plenty of others that did not.

While there was a lot of new, different and useful information in the Gnostic texts I studied, there were statements like the following ones which made me doubt that the Gnostics were the oracle of truth. I used the dialectic approach to make sense of the following three ideas of theirs that I had difficulty accepting:

THESIS: 'The egos must be observed and eliminated.'

ANTITHESIS: The ego is part of your being, when it hears you want to eliminate it then it perceives a threat.

SYNTHESIS: What happens over time as you try to work at eliminating your ego, is that mood swings become more frequent as ego tries to hijack your thinking. If you persist, parts of your ego can splinter off and bury itself deeper into your psyche and this increases the shadow side. So no, the ego should not be eliminated, there must be another way.

THESIS: 'The personality is formed in one life then discarded'.

ANTITHESIS: No one can be comfortable with the idea that you, the person you are today, is merely a container to be discarded at death.

SYNTHESIS: This creates inner confusion because you wonder where does my personality end and my soul begin? The ego automatically identifies with your personality, so again, a threat is perceived.

THESIS: 'Consciousness or essence [in a person] is a tiny part of one larger Being.'

ANTITHESIS: I don't have a problem with being a part of a whole, or a fragment of the divine essence of a larger Being. But I do have a problem with being nothing more than a brick in the wall.

SYNTHESIS: By not discussing the soul, even as a concept, you get the impression that you are a drop in the ocean with no specific identity. That may be how we started out, but it's my belief that we came into this physical reality to differentiate, to add the richness of individuality that wasn't manifest in the vast sea of consciousness called God. Otherwise God would have stayed home.

Spotting the Ego

Our spectrum of emotions tell us how we feel about anything. When we feel positive, neutral, peaceful or loving we are aligned with our Higher self (soul), but when we feel negative, cynical, angry, irritable, or indifferent (separation from others), it's a sign we are aligned with our lower self (ego). We may fall for the thinking that suffering is normal, and worse, that there is no other way. With this outlook, it's harder for the positive emotions to become our default state. It's as though they need a good reason for being there like a celebration or a victory.

Most ego emotions are those that create separation between ourselves and others. Since ego seeks approval and recognition from others, it has to deal with the maddening contradiction of needing to conform with wanting to stand out and be noticed, so ego is touchy.

Ego is overly self-conscious, controlling, insecure, and never satisfied because it's constantly comparing. You could say it's the party-pooper of life. It seeks the approval of others before oneself, and can smother spontaneous expression of a person by instilling a sense of fear of making a fool of oneself. How can ego be your true personality when it places limits on how much of your uniqueness you can express and show to others?

You can feel your ego most intently when you are in a group, any group. You will laugh when you are supposed to, and suppress any ideas that don't fit the dominating viewpoint. If someone is critical, if they dare, it's too often seen as criticism rather than another perspective or a reality check. I've had many personal experiences of this in every setting you can imagine, from home among family, with friends and acquaintances, and work in particular. Even in the prayer group I attended at my daughter's school, I had a conforming moment.

I have always believed the power of prayer is amplified when a group of people pray together. So once, at the parent prayer group, I made a request could we add one prayer at the end for a global cause, like the efforts of Amnesty International for women's rights in Afghanistan and the WSPA campaign to save bears and other animals from human exploitation. My motive came from a perception among some people that when you donate to global charities, only a small percentage of the money actually gets to those in need.

Since the group prayers we said were for the needs of our school community, I thought we could spare one small prayer for a global cause. So I put it to the group. One of the parents replied in a flash and said, in a very round-about way, that we had the authority to pray for the school community and that my suggestion was acceptable. Yet I got the distinct impression that it was not acceptable. Everyone else at the table was silent – so I couldn't tell if they were in agreement with me, or otherwise. The parent who made this assertion was not in charge, nor the leader, of the parent prayer group – there was none. Still, I decided to retreat and took it as a no. I didn't want to spoil the good will around the table so I quietly told my ego to back down, even though I felt annoyed. It wasn't too difficult for me as I'm not the type that likes to drive a point home.

Later, I tried to see it from that parent's point of view, maybe he thought the purpose of the gathering had to be respected. As it's not a religious school, the parents who organised it had to get permission, so to speak, from the school principal to use the room each fortnight. In exchange, we direct our prayers to the needs of the students and parents of the school community. I also thought the other parents may have been silent because they weren't sure about my request.

Because I didn't react with any negativity, the parent looked a bit hesitant afterwards. That doesn't mean I changed his mind, but at least my lack of ego reaction may have got him thinking.

It was a reminder to me how keeping ego under control has far more positive results. If I'd displayed any sense of irritation through my body language, facial expression, or tone of voice, then the parent who declined my request would only have focused on my negative reaction.

So the most accessible way to detect your ego is to be aware of your inner reactions to people around you. It is still useful to consider other points of view even if it's not fair or seems selfish. When you identify a selfish motive in another person you will soon realise they are operating out of fear, or the instinctive need to control, and you will feel less harsh towards them and this reduces your tension.

When you make it a habit to observe your reaction, rather than *become* the reaction, you are mediating between the outside world and your ego. It's as simple as making the choice to do so. It does take time to get to that point of awareness so that it becomes a clear choice, and only repeated attempts will get you there. It's worth persisting with, and remember, it's not about forceful effort but about will (wanting).

This is how the effort usually progresses over time:

1. You react with ego and it leaves you annoyed or irritated. A part of this reaction might splinter into resentment which may resurface at another time, or, it creates a bad mood.

2. You react with ego but realise it soon after. While still feeling the emotional dummy spit, you think of the alternatives and other points of view.

3. You react with ego, but there was a split second before you reacted when you are dimly aware of a choice, but you give in to ego because its reaction time is quicker.

4. You feel your ego's instant reaction but you swiftly decide whether to show it externally, or, let it go and process the residual feelings later.

Depending on the nature of a person's ego, this progression can take several years as it did for me. A naturally optimistic person would not take so long since their default thinking is already positive. Yet even they may find a time in their life when they struggle with a loss of faith, because everyone experiences a major challenge in their life.

The Buddhists say that instead of being attached to an outcome you should frame it as a preference instead. With attachments, you make your happiness contingent on things going your way. The subtle but powerful shift towards having preferences instead, lets you recover from disappointments far more quickly without the emotional damage that an ego attachment brings.

The sniper-like thoughts of ego will try to increase your sense of disappointment. Instead, you realize it's unrealistic to expect situations to go your way every time, or for people to be the way you want them to be, all the time. From that you can easily see that it makes no sense to wallow in disappointment when something doesn't go to plan. After all it's just the law of probability working the other way today, or, there is an important lesson or gift inside the wrapping of the disappointment.

When you remember you are a soul with ego attached, it's much easier to accept and act upon the knowing that you can shape your reality to a great extent. You can steer yourself away from thoughts that aren't helpful. A very helpful e-book called *Mind Your Mind* by Remez Sasson, a self-improvement and business success coach, discusses the power of thoughts and why we should be mindful of them:

> 'Our predominant thoughts influence our attitude and behaviour and consequently our actions. So it's very important to watch our thoughts to be careful what we think, especially those [thoughts] we often repeat.'[16]

Ego Rogues' Gallery

When ego feels under threat or insulted, it can produce a grinding feeling like you're driving over a rough gravel road instead of smooth bitumen. If I have been upset by a disappointment or unpleasant situation, I decide afterwards to put myself on auto-pilot. I keep thinking to a minimum, otherwise the mind gets agitated and overactive.

The emotion of anger releases adrenalin. It often feels like a searing type of burn in the solar plexus, or a blood boiling feeling. The subconscious mind runs the physical body, and if the negative ego is in control most of the time, it will run down a person's health in the long term. If too much adrenalin gets released with no physical outlet (like a good beefy brawl), it courses through the body like a toxin and starts to affect the immune system.

When you catch yourself going along with an ego thought that tries to remind you of an unpleasant encounter with someone and how you'll get back at them next time, stop. It's at such times I block my ego by repeating a power word over and over again until the nagging ends. Choose any word that is powerfully positive, I use words like 'abundance' or 'restore' so my ego can't get its foot in the door of my mind to force it open and come barging inside.

Ego manifests in three ways: mental, emotional, and physical. The most negative ego emotions manifest in all three aspects of our being. The following section is a rogues gallery of the most common negative ego emotions. I've chosen the negative ego faces that I personally had to tame in myself.

Arrogance

This is the selfish and vain ego, and while not being the most destructive, it is the most self-centred. It is a child of the ego of Pride which is fiercely protective of its need to be right and be respected by others. At the extreme end, it becomes absolutist and black and white with its thinking which leads to closed-minded wilful ignorance. It is unable to budge or modify its opinion even if it means others, including itself, could benefit from a different stance. This ego passionately hates to be wrong. Mahatma Gandhi once said: 'A man who always tries to maintain his dogmas in order to appear consistent, drives himself into a false position.'

Arrogance Ego symptoms

Mental: Rigid thinking, calculating, dismissive of other points of view.

Emotional: Appearing emotionless while feeling the hardness of unsympathetic reaction and righteousness.

Physical: Stiff body posture, dismissive hand movements, imperious facial expression.

Fear

Fear is the most intimidating ego of all and paranoia is arguably the most unpleasant manifestation of it. Anxiety and stress are child egos of Fear. Yet, ironically, fear is the quickest to wrestle to the ground when you fully face it.

Fear will always appear when you want to embark on something new. Take the example of a person mustering the courage to do something they are determined to overcome. When they are ready to bite the bullet, some paralysis stops them in their tracks and gives them lead feet just when they are about to start.

In this situation, all you can do is PUSH past it and ignore the feeling. The feeling does not get worse, in fact, something surprising happens. The unpleasant feeling reduces a lot or even falls away completely. It can rear its head now and then, but it becomes much easier to dismiss it each time.

This ego is a person's worst enemy when they are being watched by others. You would think ego would protect you in a way that lets you cope in the best way possible. Take a person who is naturally shy. If they have to perform in front of others it can trigger stage fright, make them visibly nervous, which affects their performance and how confident they come across.

There are physical effects like trembling, a dry mouth, butterflies in the stomach, or an ache in the gut, then thinking gets muddled (mental). The muddle-brain will trigger anxiety about not coping and losing control (emotional). This has a compounding effect and pretty soon the person is in a heightened state of stress. So ego has increased their suffering and not protected them at all.

In the self help book by Dr Susan Jeffers, *Feel the Fear and Do It Anyway*, she says the only thing we really fear, is will we cope. When you think about this statement, it makes perfect sense. It's not the challenge itself that we fear, but whether we will cope. We forget the simple truth that when a situation in the now demands it, we mostly do rise to the occasion, and even if we do botch it, the truism applies that 'What doesn't kill you makes you stronger'.

Fear Ego Symptoms

Mental: Hard to think straight, mind keeps jumping around or can't focus, repetitive obsessive emotionally charged thoughts.

Emotional: Unhappy, distressed, helpless, overwhelmed

Physical: Tension headache, lead-heavy ache in the pit of the stomach, dry mouth, nausea and loss of appetite, pale face, sweaty palms.

Anger

This is the ego that jumps you before you can make a choice about a wise response. For me, anger rips through me like a hit-and-run. Anger is an ego that is hard to lasso because it comes through the primitive amygdala part of the brain which responds faster than the brain's higher reasoning centre.

This is what I've learned: if you are in a situation where you already expressed some of your anger, leave the space or pause and take deep breaths. Wait for the peak in the feeling to pass. I found that I had it in my power to stop arguments from escalating. If you don't come back at the person, their bad manners just hangs in the air for all to see. Then it becomes easier for them to back down as well.

If you have managed to avoid an argument with someone, beware of minor irritations that occur the rest of the day, as the repressed anger may latch on to those things. You can then be like a corked bottle, until something else presses that tender button inside you, and presto...there you go again.

I was once involved in an incident where I was able to avoid a full reaction to a situation. I was at an intersection that was gridlocked in the lane I wanted to turn into, so I was over the white line when the lights changed to red. A woman to my right had to steer around me to get through, and told me off for my bad driving, and her daughter joined in as well. As they went past, I felt anger rise up from my gut like magma in a volcano. It was thick and heavy. For a split second I perceived my angry reaction to be a choice, but the ego was irresistible and I yelled something back. This was a gain because I felt my anger as part of me, not the whole of me! After the heat of the moment passed, I was able to resume my normal state of mind. It did not put me into an irritable mood.

At least my reaction was milder than what it normally would have been. What struck me later is that the ego of anger comes as a flush of a physical emotion and the mind is instantly swamped with angry come-back thoughts, and you become the anger.

For the first time, I was able to feel it in my body first and so I had a fraction of a second to decide whether to react with anger. A funny thing happened in that micro-moment of decision: I could separate thought from feeling and was able to remember there was a choice whether to retaliate or not. The fact that I finally perceived it in that split-second, made me feel like rewarding myself, so, with a 'to hell with it', I gave myself permission to yell back at them.

Jeni agreed that anger works the same way with her:

'It just comes out, with very little, if any warning.'

I had to admit:

'Yes it jumps me too. Then it's riding me like a pony. I hate it.'

I told Jeni that a good sense of the ridiculous does wonders for anger because this ego expects you to react instantly with the same seriousness. I said to her:

'I discovered this technique when my daughter was upset with me because I said 'No' to something and she came up to me to let me know it (again). She just wouldn't let it go. We were both getting angry. So I took her hands, pointed my toe and crossed one leg over the other and bobbed, stepped back, now with the other leg - like a little jig. She immediately dialled in jigging with me and the upset quickly evaporated and was replaced with giggles. Then we nearly forgot what we were arguing about.'

Anger, as a root ego, has tentacles like impatience, irritability, testiness and frustration. There are many things that can irritate a person during the course of the day like traffic, crowds, delays and excessive noise.

After blocking their reaction all day, a person may finally lose their temper at something quite small. If anger gets a person in a rope-able state by the end of the day and the person stomps around in a rage, you can be sure that person will be more prone to react with anger in another similar situation. The next time it does, it will take less to set it off. Anger is one of the ego faces that creates strong mental and emotional grooves so it's easy for it to become a default reaction.

A big part of the problem with repressed anger stems from the fact that our society is not comfortable with expressing dissatisfaction at the time, even if it's justified. The resulting emotion is suppressed. By not dealing with or releasing the emotion at some point, it simmers below the surface to fester. By that stage it is out of conscious awareness and in the subconscious. Repressed anger can slip into a person's shadow side, which then waits for a trigger that leads to rage attacks.

I was reading a local newspaper and was struck by a short news item that illustrated this. There is a recreational park that is used for multiple activities and has a bicycle track that runs through it. As usual local residents are pleading with the council to increase the access area for their particular activity, whether it's for team sports, dog walking, or cycling. There are conflicting interests that have to be accommodated.

One day, a group of residents was walking through the park from a precinct meeting, when a cyclist came around a blind corner and nearly ran into them. He managed to swerve around the group but almost knocked down a man walking on his own who was further back. The cyclist stopped, got off this bike, and hit the man across the back knocking him to the ground. Then he sped off before anyone could deal with the situation.

Anger Ego symptoms

Mental: Rapid and hostile emotionally charged thoughts.

Emotional: Ranges from irritation, hurt, gutted, seething, to outright rage.

Physical: If the anger is quickly suppressed want to double-over, trembling hands, burning acidic sensation in the blood or abdomen like poison, breathing goes shallower and a heaviness in the chest, urge to lash out with arms or legs.

Worry

Repetitive thoughts will forge grooves in the mind, so it becomes easier to think like that again. It's the same with emotions. If you make a habit of worrying, it becomes your default state, and you will start to worry even before fully weighing up the situation to see if there is anything to worry about.

Most of the things you fear might happen, never happen, they are just trouble-makers in your mind. If the thing you fear does happen, then how many times have you discovered that it was not as painful or bad as you expected, or that you coped with the situation better than you expected. Worrying is a waste of time and energy and an act of self sabotage. Be concerned, but never worry.

This is of course easy to say. But if you remind yourself how little of what you fear actually happens, you can start to end the worry habit. It's very easy to get wrapped up in things. What may seem like a big problem today isn't if you take a step back and look again with a wide-angle view, or even a week later. Taking yourself, your thoughts and your emotions too seriously leads to more unnecessary suffering.

Worry Ego Symptoms

Mental: Pessimistic thoughts like 'nothing's going right today' and 'what ifs'.

Emotional: Testiness, uneasiness, dread, anxiety, tension.

Physical: Ache or tightness in the chest, feeling heavy or sick in the stomach, a constricted feeling in the throat, tension in the jaw, cracking knuckles, for women prone to cry, for men prone to lash out.

Boredom

Ego can be a disruptor when you have to do a mundane task. You don't feel like doing it but you know that once it's done it will clear the deck for better things to do. Ego will give you feelings and thoughts of boredom, which increases the amount of effort to get it done.

In other contexts, a sense of boredom could mean that what you are doing doesn't interest you, or it's the wrong time to be doing it. So you would listen to that prompting and avoid doing the thing you hate, or doing something when you are too tired. But if it's a task that just needs to be over and done with, and you feel a resistance to doing it, then you know it's not logical to be feeling this way about it.

All work or effort has some mundane aspect to it, so your mind might be saying what a pain it is, increasing your impatience to get it done and creating tension. Once again, suspend all thoughts and come back to the moment to complete this mundane part of your work. When I do some housework, I often say mantras because housework is a no-brainer and frustrating because it's work that's never done. With this attitude, I become ripe for my ego to start a nit-picking inner dialogue. I need to make sure my monkey mind doesn't take me on a whirl-wind tour so I repeat a positive word, or set of words and, at times, dwell on their value and meaning. These days my mind is stiller and I just watch it hop more slowly from thought to thought, like a rabbit with a heavy bottom.

The type of boredom we want to be alert to is when it increases the amount of effort it takes to do a straight-forward task. For example, say you are learning to play a musical instrument. As with most things, in the early days it can be repetitive and really test your ability to stick with it. What you are trying to achieve really excites you but the ego will instil a false sense of tedium when it's nothing more than practice makes perfect.

Sometimes this boredom rouse will piggy-back on another weakness provided by your ego. For example, say you have a habit of starting things then not finishing them. You procrastinate because of the boredom trick. If you succumb to this several times, self doubt takes root and there is a risk it can bleed into other areas of your life. The boredom trick can build to a strong resistance so everything feels like, and becomes, a huge effort.

I admitted to Jeni that my grand ambition for copywriting for the web was coming unstuck, largely due to a growing resistance inside me. I didn't know what to do about it and had a stale-mate with my ego until I finally listened to my cues and dropped the whole endeavour. When you've tried to come at something from different angles and you still won't be moved, then you can only conclude that your heart wasn't in it.

Jeni said:

> 'You did mention you might be getting bored with
> copywriting. This also screams of an ego trying to

assert itself. You're the ego expert, but I know that my ego pulls this one on me all the time.'

I replied:

'Yep it's definitely ego. This internal resistance always feels the same - dread in the pit of my stomach, a kind of slowing down of myself so everything feels like an effort, flatness bordering on irritability. My mind feels drab. If this continues I'll have to conclude that it's not what I really want (sigh).'

Boredom Ego symptoms

Mental: Sluggish thoughts, difficulty concentrating, easily distracted.

Emotional: Flatness, annoyance, unsympathetic, distracted.

Physical: Dull-eyed, shaking leg while sitting, picking at face, can't sit still, sighing, slouching posture.

Negativity

When reality falls short of our expectations, the mind can resort to negativity. Before I started the ego work, I used to be plagued with negative thinking. It would jump me like a ninja and I would be hopelessly overcome. I couldn't rise above the negative thoughts and feelings so I'd become self-conscious which made me appear tense. This would affect my motor centre so at times when I spoke, my words didn't have a nice conversational flow. Physically you can look awkward as your body language gives you away. As you become pre-occupied with how you feel and how you're coming across, it gets worse. The essence of negativity is fear and self-absorption.

Negativity usually starts from thoughts before emotions, especially the inner conversation with oneself or the one liners. The expression 'monkey mind' comes from Chinese cultural writings but is often attributed to Buddha. It's a trait of the human mind to constantly move from one thing to another. If it didn't, we'd probably lose interest. It's most relentless with negative thinking because negativity is backed by fear and there is nothing more quickly disabling than fear. Negativity fed by the ego, keeps us at a lower ebb and prevents the better part of ourself coming through.

I admitted to Jeni:

'For most of my life I've been plagued by negative thinking. It has held me back, made me an under-achiever and brought me much unhappiness – all at my own hands.'

She replied:

'This sounds like a page out of my own book, out of my own life for that matter. In fact, this is something that I'm struggling with right now in my life, it seems, I've always struggled with. I've never liked myself very much, or had much faith in myself.'

We both suffered from bouts of low self-confidence, which is a child ego of negativity. I didn't have it to the extent that Jeni had of not liking myself. What I had instead was a fear of not coping, of not rising to the challenge, even feeling inadequate with no real justification.

For my personal battle with negativity, I have learned not to let a disappointment cloud my whole day. If I did that it would become easy for another disappointing thought to take root, then another. Sometimes the negativity I struggled with didn't have specific thoughts that I could confront and reject. Sometimes it was a feeling I could not explain. This would bring on thoughts to justify the feeling. This is the cascade effect that can prolong the negativity and lead to depression.

I also had to deal with irritability, impatience and testy behaviour which my husband also suffered from - so you can imagine we could, as a couple, sink into low states very quickly. Motherhood rescued me as I had a serious rethink when I realised I would be conditioning my child into the same pattern if I exposed her regularly to this way of being. Of course I am too human to simply turn over a new leaf in one day. I had to work on it bit by bit. The negativity ego face was nourished by my attention and energy for many years, so I realised it wouldn't go overnight. I put it on a slow starvation diet until now it feels like a pip-squeak.

This was difficult for me at first because the ego of indignation can be very hypnotic. Whenever I managed to be mindful in the middle of it, I'd take a deep breath and stop myself from feeding that reaction any further. It took me a few years before I could say that this type of ego reaction no longer dominates me. Since I've learned this, I've caught myself in moments of the day and thought, no, I'll try to feel compassion and tolerance for the person who just irritated me. If that's too hard, then at least feel neutral toward them. It means making the choice to not give power to the negative, which only opens the door for more suffering.

Barbara Whitfield is a spiritual author and a thanatologist (the study of death and dying). She is a recognised expert on the near-death experience. In her book, *Spiritual Awakenings*, she says:

> 'Choosing Love will free the greatest number of people. Once this understanding is gained, that each person has a choice about what they experience, people will then move very quickly. Up until now, most of humanity has been held in the grip of random emotion. Because the current spiritual teachings accept this, there is no vision to sustain the concept of Will and Choice.
>
> Even a majority of those who are dedicated to awakening, still accept feelings that rise up as a guide to their actions. Most accept feelings as something they must work through or work out, and thus remain in the hands of that trickster, the ego.'[17]

I found that you save a lot of energy if you refuse to analyse your feelings. The ego will try to make you self-absorbed with how you feel and why you feel this way. This especially applies to feelings you can't fully explain. I have told myself I feel fine when I don't, and it actually helps. It undermines the bad feeling which is expecting, and waiting, to be reinforced by negative thoughts.

When I made the decision to consciously observe my negative thoughts because I was taking on this ego face, I would be on the lookout whenever I started to have, or was having, a negative thought. These are the evolving stages I went through when I started to be conscious of my thinking and watch for negativity:

a)   You realise when you are possessed by negativity (at first).

b)   You can sense negativity creeping up on you, as you get better with (a).

c)   You can see it coming and can head it off at the pass. This is where I am with negativity, but when it comes to my ego of anger, I am still at stage (b).

Negativity is a strong bias. To neutralize it, you have to introduce the opposite bias to restore balance to your thinking. In the Gnostic work there is a process where you meditate and counter every thought with its opposite. I practiced this technique with the Gnostic group on one occasion. The format was that we'd do the exercise internally for about five minutes, then we'd each take turns to tell the others how we went with the exercise.

I had the thought 'I'm going to do this exercise well' and the immediate counter thought was 'No you're not.' Even so, it had a cancelling out effect, so the net feeling was neutral. Usually, thoughts are so fast you don't get a chance to counter-think every one of them. What works well is simply drop that thought, or stream of thoughts, like a hot potato – one after the other.

On days when I felt low or flat, I'd repeat positive words in my mind like:

'Peace Harmony Abundance Love'.

When you silently repeat words like these to yourself, on-and-off all day if necessary, it stops any trend towards a negative state and actually steers your mind towards a more neutral or positive direction.

It's a bit like steering a boat, you have to make little course corrections to keep the nose pointed straight ahead. If you fall into a negative state because something has upset you, it's not helpful to remain in that state for too long. Like quick-sand, if you bathe in the negativity and become self-absorbed, you'll sink deeper.

By refusing to feed the negative thought any further, it withers from lack of energy, and a new constructive way of thinking can be forged. It then becomes easier to default to positive. It is harder with emotionally charged thoughts but if you can do a flip in your mind, like a pancake, it's amazing how a tension seems to release inside you. Then you only need to wait for the physical effect of negativity to catch up, as that takes longer to change.

Negativity Ego Symptoms

Mental: Sour and self-defeating thoughts, overly cynical, lens of the mind narrows.

Emotional: Abrupt switches between negative feelings, inability to express feelings openly, resignation, coldness.

Physical: Heavy feeling in the body and in the chest, moving limbs seems like more effort than normal, hard to get out of chairs, tension in the face or jaw muscles.

Depression (what goes down must come up)

My depression would always stem from self-doubt that left me with dread in the pit of my stomach and an awful uneasiness in my mind. It's very common for depression to feed off fear, like when you are faced with a new challenge or overcoming one. I like someone's definition of depression as 'anger without enthusiasm'.

When I first tried to change my thinking habits that lead to negativity or depression, it felt like I was wrenching myself away from a well trodden path. It was a heave of an effort at first, but each time I tried, it became easier and easier.

Negative emotions affect the ability to think clearly and objectively. This is why negativity easily becomes entrenched and is why depression is such a common problem and so hard to disengage from. Now I am able to take set-backs or let-downs in my stride. I have come to a point where I react neutrally and quickly look for that silver lining. This takes virtually no effort on my part because I finally learned the futility of getting depressed.

Psychologist, Martin Seligman, a pioneer of positive psychology, writes that:

> 'One of the major symptoms of depression is self-absorption. The depressed person thinks about how she feels a great deal, excessively so... When

she detects sadness, she ruminates about it, projecting it into the future and across all her activities, and this in turn increases her sadness.'[18]

This makes sense as what characterises depression is repetitive victim thinking and linking one negative thought to another to cast a pall over one's entire life. There is a difference between giving expression to a feeling like sadness and letting it take over your outlook on life.

When I feel low or just flat, I try not to feed it, I even accept it. I realise that there's a reason to be feeling low on this particular day, and no more. I stop right there and avoid looking for the cause. This conscious decision has made a big impact on how long and how deeply I feel low. I realise that even if the worst thing happens, the last thing I should do is get depressed. A low state for me lasts no more than a day or two. When I've reached the lowest point of depression, and the despair feels like a form of torture, I've said to myself I will get through this, even though it seems a long way off or even impossible.

I give myself a vote of confidence. This is vital as depression often comes with a feeling that there is nothing you can do. It can also leave you dismayed which entrenches it because the person becomes depressed at being depressed. I noticed with depressive states that they seem to descend on you like a veil or a heavy feeling in the body. It's at these times I would try to lighten up and take the focus off myself. I'd get pre-occupied with something completely different and refuse to be dragged through the mud by my ego. Whenever I feel a slide into a deflated feeling, I say to myself:

'I can't afford you. You are too expensive'.

This is true really, not an opinion. Add to that a change in your body's posture which helps more than reason can find reason. Force your posture to be more upright, paste a smile on your face (yes a big false clown smile), and take several slow deep breaths. You may have noticed that it's impossible to be depressed while you are dancing. So you could try to break out into a waltz with your wife/husband, child or dog.

Depression is very sneaky and unlike other ego states which can be no more than a bad mood, depression can start out as a physical effect that lasts more than a day. Usually it's some elusive combination of experiences that cause you to turn in on yourself. For this reason I have tried to plot the most likely depression triggers from negative emotions that arise from circumstances or over-exposure to negative ideas:

- **Loneliness** {and/or feelings of isolation (whether real or perceived), not being understood or appreciated by others}.

- **Paranoia** {a very uncomfortable sensation and aligned with dread}.

- **Worry** {repetitive defeatist thinking, loss of faith in the flow of life}.

- **Sadness** or flatness {watching too much TV news, violent and vulgar movies and high-voltage in-your-face dramas}.

- **Self pity** {when coupled with remorse is a self-absorption trap}.

Jeni suffered deeper depression than I did but decided not to use anti-depressants as she felt she should take charge of her emotional state and take responsibility for her feelings. She recounted to me how depression took hold of her and how it felt. I am sure it's the same for anyone who suffers deep depression. She said:

> 'I usually feel it coming. Sadness starts creeping in and I try to push it out. I tell myself 'I can't afford you.' It really works! The sadness gets weaker. It doesn't magically disappear, but I've stopped the next stage in the trend and that is when I wrap myself up in self pity. I thought I had a really bad dose of it but it's actually helped me to stop it coming on until it becomes extreme.
>
> But there were times when I didn't see it coming. Like one morning I woke up and I felt very vulnerable, like an open wound, and I wanted to avoid contact with people because of this. I felt really disappointed with myself for waking up like this. I took your advice about not hating myself for feeling lousy which is how I would normally react. As soon as I did this, I felt something lift.'

Depression can be triggered by chronic illness and people get stuck in this terrible feedback loop. I am depressed because I feel like shit, and I feel like shit because I am depressed. I found it helps to not evaluate yourself or the situation. Instead work on a patch with some of the mental techniques discussed here and in later chapters.

Consciously try to be in the moment as much as you can and refuse to think about how bad you feel. Don't try to rationalise feelings you can't explain. This is the ego self-absorption trap. Soon you will weave your way out of it. The key is to not be expectant or impatient, but to let it flow out of you. Don't attach a thought to it so it becomes a doing thing, not a thinking thing.

Chapter 4: Ego Psychology

Freud's definition of ego was a good starting point. Yet it seemed he thought ego is all there is to us. When Jung came up with his own definition, he explained ego in the context of a Whole Self, and recognised that we are not just ego. The Gnostics explained the nature of ego as opposed to the divine spark within us. Their error was assuming that ego was multiple and externalised, as if it were a dark force. How can ego be separate from humans when ego is human?

This is why I was making progress in fits and starts with the Gnostics. Despite this, I did get many valuable insights, like realising the challenge of who has the upper hand, the soul or the ego, is the engine room of spiritual growth and that there is a distinct soul and ego identity. But it wasn't until I left the Gnostics and studied other sources that weren't rooted in religion, that I finally began to see lasting results with improving my inner state.

How to Handle the Ego

Most living things in nature are wild until they are tamed, that includes the human mind. Training the ego mind stops it being the tail that wags the dog. The Gnostic approach to ego work succeeds to a point then levels off because ego does not like words like disintegrate, eliminate, dissolve, destroy and 'dying to yourself'. Ego is by nature paranoid and defensive. Casting the ego as the opposition, or worse an enemy, would force parts of it underground to bury deeper in the psyche.

An important thing to remember is there will be times when your ego will sulk. This is just ego feeling scared because it doesn't like change. This is when parts of you are disoriented and will try to grab at anything old and familiar, like lunging towards old ways of thinking that you are trying to end. So it's a time to be kind to yourself and let ego know that you are no threat to it, that you are going to make life easier for it as well, so it no longer has to work so hard. My ego lapped up this one.

If your ego stubbornly tries to draw you back to your old predictable ways, don't give into it. If you start to get depressive feelings, flatness, or find yourself getting irritated by small things, or you feel cranky and there seems to be no reason for it, don't worry. Carry on without giving it any thought. Ego will try to distract you with low grade thoughts and feelings.

Later it may attempt to instill confusion and disorientation in you when you are making spiritual progress. This is very short lived if this does happen to you. The more common tactic it uses is to try to get you to analyse every feeling.

Sometimes we have low days with no real explanation for it and there is no use in trying to find out why. You don't want to entrench the feeling. Tell yourself:

> 'I am in a state of flux right now and whatever I feel is okay.'

How far you take ego work, and how long you spend on it, depends on your personality and ego matrix. There is no one right way. It takes dedication and honesty to get acquainted with your ego. From my own experience, I could see there was much to be gained, like:

- Stopping the worry habit,

- Increase my energy,

- Feel lighter in my body,

- Taking control of my mind to free it for more positive expression.

Ego work enables you to develop a presence of mind. That means you can take an objective view of your reactions to see if you are easing the situation or sinking yourself deeper in a problem, or even creating one. You can choose whether to identify with your ego reaction or not, and you get the ability to feel it at arms length which feels great. You discover that you have a choice and this is freedom. It's a freedom that can't be taken away by anyone else, except by your own choice.

I discovered that the ego is not my enemy, just a part of me that is backward. This was a revelation that came to me in a dream. Before my dream I had been learning the hard way not to react to ego with negativity because it will feed off that. You need to be emotionally neutral and accept, embrace and integrate the ego into your higher self. The ego's underbelly is none other than Fear, so it has to be coaxed out of the darkness into the light.

Ego responds extremely well to gentleness, acceptance, love and patience. It can be retrained but only at its own pace. If your conscious ego tries to rush it, the unconscious ego (shadow) may fight back by slowing you down with tactics like niggling doubt, hot and cold moods, lack of motivation, or procrastination.

Ego wants instant results and demands perfection. It will try to judge your efforts with thoughts like 'I should have made more progress by now'. Or it might pretend your spiritual growth is competing with other priorities of life and may shout at you 'I really don't have time for this'.

Before I started, an ego like anger would run through me like an electric current. Now I still get angry but it's on the outer edges of me. There is a core inside me that does not feel anger. I know I am getting angry but I am no longer that anger. What I found personally with ego work was that:

- It got rid of the rats in the attic (over-thinking);
- My ego thoughts are not as loud and strong;
- My mind is stiller generally, and,
- I can choose which thoughts to go along with - and that is priceless.

When I first started to practice self-awareness, I noticed that at times I could drift into a way of thinking that left me feeling flat and uneasy and could lead to a low grade depression. It could be triggered by a disappointment like not getting a job, or the opposite, winning the job but then having to endure petty office politics. It could be the experience of being let down by a friend who doesn't reciprocate. It could be recalling a memory in the past that was never resolved and something in your family dynamics reminds you of it.

I could sense this happening to me again, so one day I decided to go against my comfort zone and think the exact opposite of how I normally feel about the subject. Well an amazing thing happened. Pretty soon that slow slide to a feeling of flatness lifted and then stopped. I couldn't believe it, all from making a choice to not follow a particular way of thinking.

I asked Jeni how she experienced repetitive and negative thoughts. Sure enough, it's almost the same with her.

She said:

> 'Well... I guess it starts with thoughts creeping into my head, negative thoughts about what could happen. Then it's almost like my separate façade bodies are having a conversation.'

I replied:

> Yes I've noticed that. One ego will throw their hat into the ring, and before you know it, you are listening to a conversation in your head.

She said:

> Yes, that's exactly what it's like.

You will find the process is the same for everyone. For example, anything that is out of the ordinary or is unfamiliar, makes you suspicious before curious. The ego mind will feed thoughts to justify the suspicious feeling it has provided. More often than not, the fear wins out.

This happens when there is an opportunity to try something new. Ego will start thoughts that it might be too hard or it's risky. If it's about experiencing a new culture or meeting new people, ego can create a nervousness that you won't like something about the culture, or the people you meet will be nothing like you and you'll have nothing to say. It tries to limit your openness to new experiences.

Irrational fear is such a strong ego emotion, it will cripple us if we let it when we have to face a difficult challenge or try something new. It also crops up as irrational fear which can disorient people and cloud their judgement. The 19th century American democratic politician, William Jennings Bryan, once said 'The way to develop self-confidence is to do the thing you fear.' I had the pleasure of seeing a living example of a person who did just that.

While walking my dog one afternoon, I met a young man who had two dogs. Only one of them was on a leash. We started chatting and he told me that the one on the leash was being socialized and had 'a few issues'. He revealed to me that all his life he was afraid of dogs but he decided a year ago that he could not go on like this so he bought himself two dogs of the same breed that he was most fearful of, a kind of bull-terrier.

He seemed very relaxed with his dogs, and was determined to train and socialize the younger dog. I noticed that this dog was obeying him. I could tell from his manner that he was no longer fearful of dogs. It is a wonderful and liberating feeling to overcome your fear and discover that the object of your fear was never as bad as your own fear of it.

Another common ego tactic is when it encourages you to take offence at something. It knows how to trigger misunderstanding with others. It works like this hypothetical situation: Someone says something careless that seems to be directed at you and rubs you the wrong way. Ego steps in and baits you into interpreting it in the wrong way through a sour feeling and an unpleasant thought.

Instead of identifying with the feeling and thought, pause and take a breath. Remind yourself that if you take this personally you are giving that person ammunition to hurt your feelings. You can choose to not take it personally. Yes at first it is easier said than done, but take it from me, as someone who struggled with this more than the average person, it is well worth the effort. It doesn't matter if you only do it now and then, and the rest of the time fall into ego traps. It's never too late.

Having said that, you are left with the question - why are they being rude to you? It is a lashing out of some sort. This person is struggling with a stress, an emotional hurt, an insecurity or unhappiness, and in their emotional pain they lash out. This understanding helps to see the situation in a wider context. Ask a psychologist and they will agree that when a person is mean to another they are usually hurting inside. In most cases, they haven't really set their mind on hurting you specifically. They are probably not aware that they did, but your ego will assert that they did it on purpose.

A modern spiritual teacher who truly writes from the heart is Don Miguel Ruiz. He was born into a family of healers and raised in rural Mexico. He has brought the wisdom of the Toltecs of Ancient Mexico in his books *The Fourth Agreement* and *The Fifth Agreement*. The Toltec were not a race or culture like the Aztecs or Mayans who came later, but were a society of artists and spiritual seekers who came together more than two thousand years ago to build 'the place where humans awake and remember their divinity'.[19]

Ruiz came to spirituality after a near death experience. He wrote several books on finding personal freedom through wisdom. In his book *The Four Agreements* he speaks of why you should not let ego make you take anything personally:

> 'Whatever happens around you, don't take it personally. ... If I see you on the street and I say, 'Hey, you are so stupid,' without even knowing you, it's not about you; it's about me. If you take it personally, then perhaps you believe you are stupid. You take it personally because you agree with whatever was said. As soon as you agree, the poison goes through you and you are trapped in the dream of hell. Nothing other people do is because of you. It is because of themselves. All people live in their own dream, in their own mind; they are in a completely different world from the one you live in.'[20]

Above all, don't concern yourself with being perfect. When someone cuts you off in traffic and you instantly yell at them, or you lose your temper now and then, forgive yourself. It's always nice to stop short of a bad reaction but if you don't, it's still good to reflect on the situation soon after. I always make sure I do now. I realise I can't always react on the spot with full wisdom - hey we're only human! But the more often we back-track soon after and realise this, the more we have harvested the lesson.

Dealing with Repetitive Thoughts

Ways of thinking reveal whether we are operating from soul or ego. The most common ego state is repetitive and nagging thoughts. When we get too identified with our thoughts we'll believe anything the ego tells us. It would free up a lot of mental space if we could liberate ourselves from it. The following exercise can be tried out for about five minutes in a quiet place:

Exercise: Disposable Thought Ball

1. Position yourself in a place where you won't be disturbed. Get comfortable.

2. Sit back and close your eyes and allow your mind to buzz along as it always does.

3. Notice any repetitive thoughts that start to nag. Pay attention to where the thought is taking you.

4. Now take a deep breath and say to yourself 'Hold'.

5. Physically reach out with your hands and see yourself grabbing the train of thought as if it were a beach ball.

6. Slowly bring the beach ball towards your chest and pretend the ball is shrinking to about the size of a grapefruit, the closer it gets to your chest.

7. Hold the thought ball next to your heart for three seconds.

8. Take a deep breath.

9. On the out-breath, let out a big yell (or sound you associate with the act of releasing), and throw the ball back into the universe.

When you feel ready after doing this exercise a few times, make the physical part of this technique (i.e. reaching out and throwing the ball with your hands) a visualised command in your mind.

Exercise: Playing with Opposites

When a thought you have disturbs your peace, or induces unwarranted doubt, you can counter it with an opposite thought. It doesn't matter if that opposite thought is untrue or absurd. The absurder the better. The ego can't handle absurdity and tends to fall silent. That is because ego is convinced it is totally sensible and completely rational, so naturally it won't entertain weird or wonderful thoughts.

It's more likely that the negative thought is the one that is absurd. It makes no sense to judge a situation or person with absoluteness as the ego likes to do. Unless you were around or aware of the lead up to the situation, your viewpoint is probably subjective.

If you put an opposite thought next to an assertion you just made, then you can neutralize the thought-stream altogether. You can have fun with this. For example, say you are invited to go to a musical but you don't like musicals. You don't want to offend the person who invited you by declining the invitation, as they may be someone you are networking with, or a new friend. Ego might say:

'I hate musicals and I know I'll be bored'

The countering opposite thought could be:

'I love musicals, I want lots of colourful costumes and silly songs.'

The countering thought is meant to have a cancelling out effect so that the negative thought does not build into a negative feeling like irritation, or a visible lack of enthusiasm. Even though the countering thought is not true at all, it still works, that nagging stream of thoughts simply drops.

The Thought Eraser

While it's easier to control thinking in the day with so many distractions and inputs, it becomes a challenge when you go to bed at night. The lack of sensory input from a darkened room with your eyes closed, means the mind can be out of sync with your physical tiredness. Intrusive and repetitive thoughts can make sleep a long time coming, or wake you up with a start in the middle of the night. What you can do is create a mental eraser by repeating a simple word or image, or both.

Method 1: Neutral Object

1. Choose a positive word and a neutral image. For example, I use a single syllable word like 'peace' so my mind can make as little effort as possible. I match the word with a simple image like an apple.

2. Hold the image of the apple in your mind's eye. At the same time, repeat the word 'peace' slowly. When you say the word s-l-o-w-l-y in your mind, it makes the brain slow down.

3. Every time your mind strays from this anchor point, you stop and reel it back in like a fishing rod. Do it in a relaxed manner and don't even think about how often your mind wanders.

Method 2: Familiar Object

Alternatively, you can chose an object in your room, or a pattern on the wall:

1. Look at the object or pattern in your room and take a snapshot of it in your mind, then turn off the light.

2. While lying in bed with your eyes closed, recall the image in your mind and attach a simple power word to it like 'peace' or 'rest'.

3. Relax and let your mind wander. As soon as you get a thought that will keep you awake, interrupt it with the image of the object (like a flash card) and say the power word in your mind.

4. If you do this at regular pulses, it becomes like commercial breaks that will chop up your concentration on the thoughts that are keeping you awake.

Method 3: Let Go Thoughts

If you've had a very hectic day and your mind is over-stimulated, emotionally charged thoughts are harder to release, so you can tell every one of these pop-up thoughts, or stream of thoughts:

> 'Thank you. I will think these thoughts later, I wont forget.'

...and release the thought.

Method 4: The Cradle

A friend of mine who sometimes suffers insomnia has a technique that cuddles herself to sleep. She imagines she is in the hollow of a large tree, or a warm cave all curled up like a hibernating bear. I have tried imagining I am a newborn baby in a pram being taken for a walk and the bumping caused by the ruts in the footpath, and flickering daylight, lull me to sleep.

The later chapters of this book also have a range of exercises which you can select to try out or use when the need arises. Don't forget the more general tips and exercises in other chapters too. As you apply these strategies on your ego, it becomes easier to spot those ego tactics and not be overrun by them.

Ego Can Set up a False 'fork in the road'

It is ego that tries to erode ambition whenever you want to try something outside your comfort zone. It will go along with the idea until you start to make moves towards the goal. When the time comes to actually doing it, you may get an uncomfortable feeling in the pit of your stomach and thoughts of insecurity. How can this be? You were fired up about it only a day ago, but when your idea intersects at the point of action, you suddenly feel anxious and worrying thoughts pop into your head and this induces hesitation.

When you hesitate it makes you feel uncertain, then you start to doubt your resolve. This is the trap. The ego can encourage indecision, or procrastination, and a stalemate results. In some cases, you are left with the illusion of a fork in the road. This happens with minor or major choices. A minor example is a type of stage fright I get, which I discovered to my amazement that my husband also gets.

This is another example of ego being the same in every person, even in people with very different sensibilities. I get nervous just before installing new software on my computer and will put off doing it, even though I made the decision to buy it and know why I want to install it. When we bought our very first home computer back in 1992, an Amstrad, it sat in the box for a month before we opened it. For some reason we both felt this stage fright even though there was no risk involved.

Take a more goal-oriented example, one morning you might decide to do that meditation exercise you planned to do. Then you suddenly get an urge to sort through the old photo albums you've been meaning to do for ages. You decide on the photo albums. While you are doing this task ego reminds you that you just said no to your spiritual exercise, and tries to instil feelings and thoughts that maybe you are not so interested in it after all.

It then appears to be sensible by asserting that you don't really have the time for it anyway. You start to feel opposition, so the next time you have a choice to do your meditation, it will be easier to decide against it again because now you may doubt your own sincerity.

There is a decoy at work here. Remember that it's possible to create the idea of an opposition when there isn't one. When you get this idea that you have an opponent, a conflicting choice, or a decision to make, you give it legs. You may have to face a task or situation that you are not relishing. Ego will mask itself as hesitation and boredom with the thought 'I really don't feel like doing this now.' It will reinforce this thought with a flat feeling, or the feeling comes before the thought.

Instead, and this is the trick, say to yourself, 'Okay this time my urge to do the photos wins out but I can apply myself to the task in a meditative way, focus on the now, while doing it.' You probably will anyway as looking at old photos will draw you into a reverie. You go with your urge knowing you will do that meditation exercise after or later. It is important to go with your clear urges because that is when you are being sincere and it's the right time. But you do draw a line with procrastination that wants to repeat itself.

In working with ego there are no absolutes, so it pays to be open to your intuition and your urges. It could be that the persistent attitude you are feeling towards something may not be ego-based. Say you are repeatedly feeling resistance towards something even though your mind thinks you must move in that direction. This could be a time when a part of you is saying 'not now'. Your higher self will give you urges that will inspire you to follow the path of least resistance. It will prod you when the time is right, and when a situation is optimal to take advantage of now. On the other hand, it may signal when not to act to protect you from danger or disappointment.

Yet there are times when you don't have an urge to help you. For example, you are in a position to grant a favour for someone. If you start to get too preoccupied with the choice, ego can take advantage of your over-thinking by making conflicting assertions. One ego voice might say it's not your responsibility anyway, and the other voice says, you are letting someone down if you don't offer to help. This only puts negative pressure on you. Yet another ego thought can feed you the feeling that you are being put upon and this adds to the inaction.

When you have what seems like two conflicting ideas in your mind, don't think of it as a decision you have to make. Wait with an open mind to see which idea wins out on this occasion. If you go with one and not the other, let yourself know there will be time for the other. But if you do feel unsure, either in your head or body about this, immediately picture in your mind's eye that you are facing yourself and say:

'I can accommodate both choices at the right time.'

This way you are not attached to a specific choice or outcome but put trust in your higher self to steer you in the right direction at the right time. When you consciously decide not to take a knee-jerk reaction, or go into a tug-of-war about choices, your ego may step in and start to criticise. If that doesn't work, it may present an imaginary dilemma. It can provoke thoughts that you're at a fork in the road, that there is a decision to be made like an either/or situation.

My spiritual friend, Jeni, wanted to devote more time to practicing spiritual techniques when she was starting to write her children's book. She got it into her head that she had to choose between the two. There was no decision to make because neither were in conflict with the other and one did not depend on the other, but her ego had created a tug-of-war in her mind. She wanted to write the children's book with spiritual overtones. Her ego created a duality saying that she couldn't write the book, and, take up spiritual growth at the same time. Her ego confused her into thinking she had to make a choice between the two, like she had come to a fork in the road.

Her ego was asserting:

'It's time they are two separate entities. It has come to a point where each is holding the other back.'

This was the logic it used. So for months she got stuck and did not progress with either of her goals. This increased her stress and led to a loss of confidence. She brought her stale-mate out into the open in one of her emails to me:

> 'I'm putting forth a half effort on both, especially my book. In fact, both have come to a screeching halt in the past few months. It's like my existence is on hold or in neutral, until I make a decision.'

But are they separate? Taking up spirituality as a way of life, or as a mindset, does not mean it steals time from your regular and normal pursuits. You still do the regular things in your life but you make them the vehicle for spiritual growth. This can be as simple as keeping your mind on track while you are doing something, or not falling into a day-dream when doing something routine.

Jeni said at one point, 'the more I think about it' which means she was over-thinking. The next analytical thought is that you're at a fork in the road. Yet it was the ego that created this juncture. Jeni's book and her spiritual growth can co-exist because for now the book is a vehicle for spiritual growth, just like anything you are devoting most of your time towards. Contradictory thinking like this causes doubt that leads to indecision, and that leads to inaction.

In times like these the only way to get out of this impasse is to 'just do it'. Don't plan, don't analyse, just start. I take this approach with anything I do, it's made all the difference as I would tend to over-think as well. It's amazing how things fall into place when you trust yourself and just start, then after starting, take the next step, then the next step. Once it becomes more routine you'll start to notice a flow and ego backs down – a lot.

Ego Facades put Barriers Between People

The most common way ego will try to alienate people is through resentment and grudges. When someone slights us, acts inconsiderately and doesn't behave according to our ego dictates, we assume that person was doing it deliberately to hurt or insult us. This could be when they don't return a smile, walk right past us without saying hello, or act in a manner that signals to our ego that they don't value us. The effect of incidents like this is reinforced by all the stored unconscious resentments our ego remembers from similar situations in the past.

A negative reaction occurs the same way for anyone in these types of situations – an uncomfortable feeling then negative thoughts to explain the feeling, then justifying the negative thoughts. I told Jeni about the difficulty I had of dealing with people who seemed to have an opposite value system to me.

One person may never think to brag or show off, but another thinks it's quite normal. Bragging does not actually harm anyone unless you let it. When I was in a situation like this, I thought it would be helpful to dig a bit deeper because if I didn't have this quality myself, it would not bother me. I would see it for what it was, and be able to dismiss it.

I admitted to Jeni that I was dealing with cynical feelings about a person who was bragging about their material success.

It annoyed me because my own value system knows that bragging is not important, yet I would still get affected.

I said to her:

'...but I wonder why does it bother me so? Why can't it be 'water off a duck's back'?.... I've soul searched and asked myself am I envious in some way? What do you think? I get so irritated by their talking-up and their showing off. But why does it annoy me? Why can't I just be unaffected?'

She replied:

'Is it possible that you're jealous and want their approval? I believe, at least for me, that's where the annoyance comes from. It also sounds like pride. At some level, I feel like they look down on me for not living like they do. While I shouldn't care what they think, my pride gets hurt because their bragging makes me feel like I'm not good enough. I take their bragging as a personal snub on me. Even though I know better, I immediately put up a front and feel defensive.'

Jeni's description of her ego reaction in this type of situation is exactly like mine. I too take it as a snub and feel like putting up a front. That's one simple example of how ego is the same in all of us and creates misunderstandings just like a hall of mirrors.

Let's look at a hypothetical example that is more complex. Say a person is newly promoted and may feel like they have to continually prove themselves. They become sensitive to criticism and find it hard to delegate to others and trust them enough to give them autonomy. I have seen working relationships unravel over mutual misunderstandings similar to this. Let's explore this scenario:

Say team leader, Brad, is not sure about a team member's sincerity after he failed to meet a deadline. Josh gives assurances that it won't happen again but Brad doesn't completely want to give the benefit of the doubt because Josh is not someone he especially likes, only tolerates. Brad may harbour doubts, so when he communicates with Josh, his posture, tone of voice and manner seem to reflect that doubt.

Josh notices and starts to feel less confident around Brad. This lack of confidence becomes obvious to Brad who sees Josh's awkwardness around him as a lack of enthusiasm. Brad starts to avoid Josh and relates to him in an offhand way.

Josh's feelings around Brad make him overly sensitised to the lack of faith Brad seems to have in him, so he unconsciously starts to withdraw his effort and the quality of his output declines. Brad observes Josh is not putting out his best and now thinks he may lack the ability.

Josh, feeling the lack of support, makes mistakes and so Brad feels like he was right about Josh all along. Brad feels the power of being right, but was he? Or did they both sow the seeds for disappointment?

This is another one of ego's mechanisms to put barriers between people. No one opens up to the other so misunderstandings compound. Jerry Hirschfield in his book *My Ego, My Higher Power and I*, offers this understanding of ego's divisive nature:

'The ego can't conceive of our being whole. It cannot comprehend wholeness because of its linear, sequential nature, it can only concentrate on small pieces at a time. To derive a feeling of comfort, it must divide, conquer and control.'[21]

This explains why Brad and Josh were both absolute with their thinking about each other. Brad was sure he was right about Josh, and Josh was sure that Brad wasn't nice.

Ego creates barriers within a person, like contradictory personality traits that confuse others. This is usually when a person's behaviour or attitude is not consistent. A close friend related to me one day:

'It's almost like my Dad has a split personality. While there is always tension between us no matter what, he is much more pleasant to be around when it's just my family. His whole personality and attitude completely change when my sister and her family are around.'

Some people are so dominated by their ego, that when they are in the grip of one ego face and it stops, another will take over. By the end of the day they are emotionally and physically exhausted. There's a Star Trek Next Generation episode that illustrates this very well. The episode is called *Sarek*. It's about a Vulcan diplomat who's getting old and has started to suffer a degenerative disease where Vulcans slowly lose control of their emotions. You may recall Vulcans from the original *Star Trek* series (Spock was one). They are an alien race who have learned to suppress their emotions and consciously only express logic. But ecause they are humanoid they never actually got rid of these emotions. So when they get seriously ill the feelings they've been suppressing all their life come to the surface. It's extremely distressing for them as they experience it as a loss of dignity.

This Vulcan diplomat was aboard the *Enterprise* star ship for an important negotiation of a treaty. He was in the grip of his illness and his minders were worried he wouldn't be able to pull it off. The Captain suggested they do a mind meld together so the Vulcan diplomat could off-load his emotional baggage and be free of it for the negotiations. Of course after this event they would mind meld again so the Captain would return the emotions (ego) back to the Vulcan. The mind meld took place and while the Vulcan diplomat was able to do his work with a clear head, the poor Captain had to retire to his room and sit through the ego attacks. There's a scene where he experiences each ego face, one after the other. He starts with anger, fear, pride, arrogance and so on with all the physical and emotional traits that characterise them, including the things he says, the mutterings, the shouting, tortured expressions, postures of indignation and scorn, then crying and sorrow – the works! I have to say Patrick Stewart is a fine actor and what he had to portray is an actor's dream.

When the nature of ego is not understood, a person will assume it is all they are. They let ego control their thinking and their outlook. Ego is linear so it doesn't like to reconcile two opposing ideas and contradictory personality traits. This limitation can create a tug-of-war in a person's mind leading to indecision. It keeps people at less than their optimal capacity as it's a wrong use of their conscious energy.

Training your ego is a labour of love. The more balanced and whole you become, the better you are to those around you so they have a chance to improve as well, or at least bask in your light. It is like a gift that can be shared. Ego will not mind being trained as long as it doesn't see a threat to itself. For all its slyness and negativity, ego wants nothing more than to be loved and accepted. Because ego is backward, the treatment for it is in reverse. Normally you would give love when it is earned. In the case of ego, you accept and embrace it, first. In the next chapter, we start the ego work with methods for training the ego and managing it day to day.

You can make ego work an inner adventure, not a commitment that makes you feel obligated. Cast yourself as a character that you are going to work upon to groom and recruit in life. The world is a stage and you can be the director of the actor called you. You have so many fine qualities that need more room for expression and haven't reached their full potential yet.

Chapter 5: Ego in Training

The first step is to recognise that you are more than just your ego. It took me time to come to grips with the idea that it's ego that creates suffering, then I realised my ego is not the real me anyway. It's like an impostor who wants to take centre stage and won't leave me in peace. If I feel irritated and try to get over it quickly, an unpleasant feeling in my gut rises up to insist that I stay irritated. The ego can be sly so take your time to get to know your ego's ways.

Ego is God-fearing and is the part of us that suffers and creates its own suffering. Some people with tougher egos may experience emotional pain when they first try ego work. It is still worth persevering as the rewards are far greater than anything money can buy. You don't need to have an intention to surrender your ego as it will happen quite naturally and often unconsciously.

If you find yourself experiencing an emotional see-saw one day when you start to train your ego, this can be an encouraging sign. This is ego trying to rock your boat to see if you will tip out. Ego will want you to get frustrated with yourself so you are ripe for more self sabotage. This is why you should never give too much thought to what causes you to suddenly lose your cheer one day. Everyone struggles with it, it's a natural human condition.

Use a diary to journal your inner adventures. This can be a dream diary, a note of your meditations and how you went, or a daily diary where you jot down some observations. At some point you will want to record some of your eureka moments, synchronicities or strange coincidences and profound experiences. Talking about profound experiences, one of the diversions ego uses is that, as time goes by, it acts like what happened last month is no longer relevant - that it happened so long ago, you must have been dreaming. Watch for this.

Writing about your conquests, or otherwise, will have two benefits. Writing side-steps the ego tactic of making the passage of time dim the impact of your memory. Once you keep a record of your experiences, the ego can't distort the memory. I have to say though, that on the spiritual path there are some experiences that can never be forgotten, but even those should be recorded confidentially.

Defining your Personal Boundary

Sensitive and empathic people have a difficult time drawing a boundary around themselves. In families, mothers are automatically in an empathic role being the carers and nurturers. It's often mothers who get run down from neglecting their needs for the sake of their family members. It's healthy to push back on others' needs now and then so they don't bleed into your own space, and before you know it, you are in service to them emotionally or psychologically without a break.

Empaths, in general, can easily feel for or identify with other people's suffering. They also get overwhelmed if they remain around boorish or insensitive people for too long. Without meaning to, they also collect vibes from people but can't work out whose is whose - is it me or the other person? The way to tell if an impression you get is yours or someone else's, is to see what residual feeling you have left after you leave the situation. If the vibe you get is sudden and totally unexpected, be it negative or positive, and it doesn't linger very long with you, then I suspect it is coming from that person.

We do communicate telepathically, without our knowledge, so it can be difficult to tell if it's your reaction, or, your feeling is being met in the middle by the other person. If you can't work it out, don't try. If you are determined, then ask yourself 'Is there any reason I would feel this, or think this?' If the answer is no, then assume you picked up the feeling/idea from someone else.

The late Dr Joshua Stone, a transpersonal psychologist and founder of the Melchizedek Synthesis Light Academy, was one of the leading spokespersons for the Planetary Ascension movement which is dedicated to accelerating the spiritual evolution of humanity. He said when you develop self boundaries it becomes easier to set healthy boundaries with others:

> 'Without healthy self boundaries one cannot choose one's life for one's programming ends up choosing it for them. ... the subconscious mind,

having no reasoning, will ultimately run ones life into the ground if you let it for it was never designed to be the computer programmer just the computer....If one does not have boundaries one will react to life instead of respond.'[22]

There are ways to strengthen the personal boundary like meditation that includes the conscious closing of one's aura to outside influences. If your days are busy and it's difficult to schedule time for meditation, try the following self affirmation exercise which only takes a minute.

Exercise: Drawing your personal boundary

After you wake up in the morning and get out of bed, try this little exercise to get you on a good note for the day.

1. Stand tall with your feet slightly apart and raise your arms high as if touching the ceiling.

2. With arms still high, stretch your spine gently as if you are trying to make yourself taller and splay your fingers. Take a deep breath and exhale.

3. Drop your arms by your sides and say:

    'I am centred in my being and at peace with myself.'

    *This says you are aware of the three parts of your being –
    conscious, subconscious and super conscious -
    and have acknowledged ego.*

4. Now declare:

    'I love myself unconditionally.'

    *Stops you from hooking your happiness on
    getting approval from others.*

5.   Assert to yourself:

'I own my personal power at all times.'

Helps you gather courage to protect your boundary and be assertive instead of defensive, if the need arises.

6.   Say to yourself with hand over the heart:

'I change my attachments to preferences.'

Placing your hand over your heart shows ego that you respect the emotional stake you have in the attachment. Buddha said in the 'Four Noble Truths', that all suffering comes from attachments.

The last step is optional:

7.   Say the *Circle of Protection* conjuration three times. (in Chapter 6 - Being Your Higher self).

This will seal and protect your aura from other people's negativity, including your own.

Quick Tips for Managing Your Ego Every Day

You may be unsure whether you really need to train your ego. It doesn't matter if your ego is not that stubborn or tough, everyone can benefit from ego work because everyone is tested in their life one way or another. It will be ego that will let you down because it responds with fear and this creates the pain and suffering experienced when we face uncertainty, divisive challenges, difficulties or change.

The exercises and advice in this book are meant to be applied selectively according to your own needs and desires. As I said earlier, there is no one single right way to do it and it remains your choice how far and deep you want to take it. If it still feels very new to you, then the following general tips can be applied like a tester to see how well you respond and that way you can gauge your interest and level of commitment to ego work.

Tip 1:   Be in the moment and stay in the NOW

Limit day dreaming as much as you can because that's one of the main entry points ego uses to feed off your psychic energy. When you dwell on the past or worry about the future, the ego easily takes charge and feeds you endless replays and scenarios. This distracts you and makes anything you do take longer to complete and increases the chance of making mistakes.

Tip 2:   'Feel the fear and do it anyway' (Dr Susan Jeffers)

I've always loved that saying coined by Susan Jeffers. If you have to face something that is creating fear inside you then DO push past the fear even if your hands are trembling and your gut aches. These physical effects are a ruse by ego, I discovered this for myself. Remember that sometimes the only way out is through. Unless it's physical danger you are facing, all fears are worse than the thing feared, and will quickly fall away like a dead skin when you face it square on.

Tip 3: Don't go along with every thought

When you stop yourself from over-thinking, the ego will not have as many hooks. It is always dropping suggestions into your head to get a train of thought going. And it's always small minded talk that chatters like a monkey. If left to run riot, it creates enough noise in your mind that inspiration and creativity gets choked off.

Tip 4: Don't compare yourself to others

Stop as soon as you become aware you are doing this. Ego wants to find reasons for you to feel superior to others, or the flip side, feel intimidated by others. A more useful way is to compare yourself to yourself by asking have I done to enrich my life?

Tip 5: Find a book on emotional strength

I recommend this book to learn more about negative emotions and how to not have them running you: *Emotional Freedom - Liberate Yourself from Negative Emotions and Transform your Life* by Judith Orloff MD.

Tip 6: Don't beat yourself up for making a mistake

It's not how many mistakes you make that counts but how you handle them, what you learn from the experience, that's what counts. It's that old saying, you learn more from failure than you do from success.

Tip 7: Allow those low moments without worrying unduly

I came to a conclusion that it's not normal to be chirpy and upbeat every single day. Let's face it, this world is not an easy place to endure sometimes. Some days you are more sensitive. That's how I see it.

Tip 8: Show your vulnerability sometimes

It breaks the ice between you and others and is universally appealing. It makes you and others feel less alone and encourages them to reach out with sympathetic feelings like understanding, compassion, warmth and generosity.

Tip 9: Make self-awareness a mental habit

It's a valuable habit to observe your mental and emotional reactions. It means you are not identifying with every thought that comes into your head. By all means go along with an encouraging and happy thought, but any thought that makes you feel uneasy or unhappy, let those drop from your mind. This is especially true for emotionally charged thoughts.

Tip 10: Let Go and Let God

Jeni once said 'An ego will take over and I just let it. I don't fight it like I should.' Yes I understand, but fighting doesn't work. It digs its heels in, or another ego takes its place. I now acknowledge the ego thought or feeling, thank it, and then release it. This seems to work far better. In fact it works like magic.

Tip 11: Be prepared for ego resistance at first

You might have some resistance from your mind when you try to change your thinking patterns. The mind isn't used to having its habits changed, even if it's beneficial.

Don't be discouraged by your ego's stubbornness, it won't last. Just quietly substitute your negative thoughts with positive thoughts. You don't need to analyse why you are thinking or feeling a certain way. It's better if you don't, as this is a lure of the ego.

Remez Sasson in his e-book, *Mind Over Mind*, makes a very similar observation:

> 'This resistance will manifest in different forms, as forgetfulness to substitute negative with positive thoughts, as doubts about the usefulness of doing so, and as laziness and procrastination. Continue working on your thoughts and attitude without giving up. Your persistence will eventually conquer the resistance of your mind.'[23]

If you decide to take up ego work (ongoing), there may be times you feel like you are being tested. Take it as a good sign. Your ego would not be in a panic unless you were making progress. In time the ego's resistance will slow down and shrink. It's important not to judge yourself if you feel you aren't making much progress. What's important is that you are trying, and most importantly, want to try. If you do find yourself in a struggle you'll always turn that corner when you least expect it, but only after you let go of expectation, and there'll be no looking back.

If your will to change for the better is strong, that does help enormously as the effort required becomes much less and is driven by pure desire instead. Often the growth within you happens subconsciously and you are changing without realising it. Later it dawns on you when you see you are able to take more pleasure in the little things in life and not get so affected by life's let-downs. Life becomes richer as you attract more of what you want as a result of releasing yourself into the flow of life by letting go ego's need to control. You also start to feel lighter in your body which is a real treat.

Staying Positive in Testing Times

There are two arenas in life where a person's ego is challenged mercilessly. That is in family and in work. There are egos that only crop up in family situations because we are less bounded by social norms and we know our family love us unconditionally. With work, we can become over-identified with our role and this can bring out ego behaviour that has no outlet anywhere else.

There are times when situations arise that seem to test our mettle. It's these times that are opportunities (in disguise) for healing and growth. You can work on that part of yourself that's had a tendency to made life harder for you. Try to remember to observe your suffering, not just suffer it, and use the experience to shed light on your ego faces. I've done this myself and it does take the sting out of the hurt and you get to know yourself a lot better.

During the dialogue I had with Jeni we would refer to struggle and battling the ego, then we both realized we were making a rod for our backs. She said at one point:

> 'I'm just tired of the constant battle and want it to be over. It's just so draining.'

We wondered why our progress seemed to be one step forward, then two steps back. Around this time, I had a dream about embracing and accepting the ego instead of resisting it. I told Jeni and we concluded that we had to recast the whole effort we were making towards ego work. If you think of it more like an exercise in ghost-busting or another metaphor that turns it into a game, it does change the experience profoundly. Sure it can feel like a battle at times, but that is ego's attitude trying to magnify the effort. To think of it as a battle or struggle, makes your spiritual growth just that, because it means you agree with ego's opinion.

When ego resists because it thinks you are fighting it, this can increase the risk that you may abandon spiritual growth altogether because you may form the belief that it's too hard. Before Jeni and I came to this realization, we had a see-saw of a time with our ego work. Jeni once said:

> 'Mine seems to be extra stubborn lately, like it's fighting extra hard. I am having a hard time saying no to it. I seem to like the ideas it comes up with. I'm used to giving in to it, and am not sure I know how to say no or have the ability to say no.'

I replied that the reason it's extra stubborn lately is because she was making spiritual progress. I was happy for her in a way because it validated my experience since I was going through the same thing. The ego gets alarmed and worries you want to do away with it. It is not easily convinced, and only time and consistency erases its worry. So don't get discouraged.

Ego will stubbornly try to make you self-absorbed, but if you jump outside yourself and take a second look at all the good things in your life, you can stop this from happening. By refusing to be self absorbed, the ego has no real edge to manipulate you. If you stick by this decision, it helps enormously with the internal power shift that's gradually taking place inside you – from ego to soul.

If you caved into ego more times than you care to admit, just pick up the pieces each time and learn from the experience. It's not a game of three strikes and you're out. The only part which takes effort (in the beginning) is remembering to stick to your resolve. Eventually that resolve turns into a driven desire once you see the gains you can make. Just realise that there are no quick fixes or silver bullets. If there were, it would be a superficial fix and would only mask the problem and we have plenty of those.

To train ego permanently, it means working with it in your normal day to day settings because this is when ego's guard is down. Taking time out to attend a weekend workshop retreat or committing to an intensive boot camp program of a few days does boost morale but will not produce lasting results. This is because ego is master at pretenses and appearances. Because it's a staged event, ego would hide behind one of its many masks. It would seem to be cooperating with you and you'd feel triumphant as you would see quick progress and small victories. When life returns to normal, you would be back to where you started as ego leaps at you from behind the mental bushes of your mind, happy to take you by surprise.

For this reason the work with ego is to change nothing on the outside, but instead, make use of the settings, situations and people in your life right now. They are all vehicles available to you to practice self-awareness, observation, and ego training techniques. If there are things in your life that need to be changed or be rid of, then those things will change or go away as a side-effect caused by the positive change in you. As the ancient Chinese Taoist teaching from the *Tao te Ching* says:

> 'He is ready to use all situations and doesn't waste anything. This is called embodying the light.'

Naming your Ego Faces

When you get a situation in life that seems to test your mettle, this is when ego has a chance of wresting control. It is also a time when ego is most hypnotic. It is like a test to see how attached you are to ego demands. When I had a major ego challenge in the work place, I was experiencing emotional pain (described in the case study in Chapter 7 – Mentoring Your Ego). It was wearing me down and I needed a break-through. The egos I had at work had a characteristic feel about them. They weren't like the ego faces I get in other settings.

Out of frustration, I started to put a name to the ego faces so I could isolate and name the ego feelings. This helped me put a boundary around the swirls of negativity and self-defeating thoughts I was having. Through the backwash of my emotions, I discovered more about my ego that I needed to work on and turned the whole struggle into a game. After I labelled my ego faces, I then used some of the ego training techniques on them individually. I highly recommend you try this out as it can be fun, funny and at the very least, provide you with an exposé of yourself.

These are the ego faces I was able to identify and name at the time of my major ego challenge:

Crushing Self Doubt (CSD)

Once, a family member made a throw-away line that I was goofy and soon after I felt this ego slowly gnaw away at my self perception. I repeated some power words to stop it from going further. I know where that feeling normally takes me and for once I could see it at arms length. It's that feeling that threatens your sense of self-esteem like 'suppose I throw a party and no one shows up' type of feeling-thought.

I've Been Wronged (IBW)

This is the 'poor me' ego we all get at one time or another that is responsible for entrenching a person into a victim mind-set. This one manifests as a tight or heavy feeling in my gut and an unpleasant atmosphere in my mind about 'why me', 'I've had it'. A throw-in-the-towel sort of thinking, and feeling like I am about to burst into tears.

Defensive (DEF)

This is the outwardly visible ego. It comes out as anger and leads to petty arguments. Or it becomes a strong urge to lash out at people around me who I believe have done me wrong (yes, also feeds into IBW ego). I need to set them straight with a few strong words but because I am emotional, I can't form my words in a constructive way and it comes out as a counter-attack. Since I worked on this ego, it feels much smaller. It used to come with a grinding acidic feeling in my stomach. When angry, it felt like my blood was poisoned or boiling.

Nobody Likes Me (NLM)

The working landscape in office life can be ripe for ego clashes, misunderstandings and ego trips. This one only appeared at work and was quite strong. I would easily get the false impression that people were avoiding me and that I was being deliberately excluded. It could also double-up with the CSD ego. I would revert into myself and start to have isolating thoughts.

Ms Feisty Gone Sour (FGS)

This ego wants to shoot from the hip, blow something up (verbally). It can arrive after IBW and DEF. It is the last one in the pack, but doesn't always show up. It likes to strut out scenarios of me saving the day and getting satisfaction. It also comes with feelings of some type of come-back to the person, or persons, involved. Usually dramatic, it makes me look powerful and heroic with everyone feeling ashamed of themselves in my wake. Lots of presumptions about what is said and what the counter-responses will be, I would do this and I would say that, but none of it comes true.

Self Sabotage (SS)

Because of the ego challenge I experienced, I finally saw the pattern in me that this treacherous ego has spun all my life. It goes like this:

1. Something good, positive or encouraging comes into in my life (an opportunity).

2. At first I see it as an opportunity, a stroke of luck or lucky break.

3. I start to fantasise about how I can take advantage of this opportunity.

4. When I hit an obstacle that seems to threaten to burst my bubble, I start on this train of thought along the lines of 'it's too good to be true'.

5. This leads to doubtful thinking till it reaches a point where I believe I was deluding myself and there was no opportunity after all.

6. Without realising it I have dealt myself out of the opportunity.

Bottom's Falling Out of Everything (BFO)

This is the panic stations ego. It's the one that makes you wild-eyed when you can't find something you are desperately looking for, like realising you forgot to make a mental note about where you parked your car in the multi-storey car park. Normally your rational mind steps in as you tend to know it's interfering with your survival so it's usually dealt with on the spot after a few expletives have been said. I try to nip this one in the bud, using intelligence, as this ego feels immature and silly to me.

I shared my ego mapping with Jeni who replied:

'It's amazing! I feel like you are describing me when I read these ego descriptions... I didn't realize egos in different people were so similar. I remember you once said that everyone has the same egos. This just may prove it.

For me, DEF and IBW feed into one another and NLM and CSD feed into each other. In the end, all of these come down to one feeling - FEAR. They are all different ways to manifest fear: NLM-fear of not being loved; DEF-fear of being attacked; IBW - fear of being ignored; CSD-fear of failure.'

I couldn't agree more.

Chapter 6: Situational Ego Training Exercises

Apart from the mind exercises given so far, the method of ego work is mostly situational. This means that instead of making the time for it, you use the situations in your everyday life as the vehicle. By using all the situations that happen and encounters with people you have to observe your ego reactions, you use your life as the matrix for spiritual growth.

Over the years, I have developed and tested on myself the following ten situational ego training exercises. They came about through personal challenges that seemed to arrive at my doorstep and I recognised them as opportunities for growth. They have helped me and actually work when done with sincerity and repetition. Use them when the need arises. You can do them out loud or silently in your mind. They work best if you repeat the technique until you feel relief.

1. When in the Grip of an Ego

At times you don't always see the ego coming until it's on top of you creating disharmony or discontent. Jeni confided to me how at times she dealt with a rising damp of sadness:

> 'I usually feel it coming. Sadness creeps in and, I can push the sadness away. I tell myself 'I'm not going to put up with you today.' It absolutely works. The sadness goes away, not magically, but the black shell I've wrapped myself in cracks and slowly falls away.
>
> But, sometimes, like this last episode, it doesn't work, or I don't see it coming. This last time, I sort of woke up one morning and found myself in the deep end of the pool, with cement shoes on. I have followed your advice about letting myself feel lousy without analysing it. As soon as I stopped beating myself up over it, I felt the shell begin to crack.'

Even if you feel you spotted the ego too late and you're right in the thick of it, these two techniques will greatly reduce or stop the ego's effect.

Exercise: I couldn't take another bite

1. Imagine in your mind's eye someone is giving you a second helping of food, but you're already full and had enough.

2. Imagine the food on the plate is the negative thoughts and unpleasant feelings that's gripping you right now.

3.   Imagine you are pushing away this plate which is piled high with food. It could be mashed potato and the portion is really gross.

4.   You don't want to offend ego, so you say: 'Thank you, but I couldn't take another bite.'

Exercise: Face off with Love

This technique is effective if you have an unpleasant feeling but the thoughts to justify it have not yet formed and taken root.

1.   Go somewhere where you can be private and quiet for about two minutes.

2.   Take a deep breath, close your eyes and still your mind.

3.   Now ask yourself gently 'What's wrong?' and 'Is there anything wrong?'

4.   Be still, don't think, and wait without expectation.

5.   If no answer comes, ask this feeling to step forward and come into the light.

6.   See yourself smiling and nodding in understanding to this ego feeling.

7.   If you still get silence (usually the case, as ego may not fess up), nod your head and smile like you understand anyway.

8.   Say to yourself 'I really appreciate you caring, and I thank you very much.'

9.   Take a deep breath, and as you exhale, pretend that you are letting go of the feeling.

2. Feeling Irritated by Others

We tend to have people in our lives that are capable of pushing our hot buttons. When another person has rubbed you the wrong way, there may be hard feelings after the encounter, but remember that person cannot have that effect on you unless you had some of that quality in yourself.

This may be hard to believe but I will give you an example of myself. I acknowledge that I'm not the tidiest of housewives so when my in-laws have exclaimed in a certain tone of voice 'Wow your place looks tidy', I've taken it as a compliment. Most women would see it as sarcasm – but I don't, because having a tidy home all the time is not my priority.

Now that's not the case with things I haven't admitted about myself, and it's these things that get to me. But otherwise, it's so true that you would not react to something said if that thing had nothing to do with you, or wasn't a part of you. As the Gnostic master Samael Aun Weor said, 'We must use the errors we see in others for our own self discovery.'

Exercise: Mirror Mirror

This technique is done after the person who irritated you has left your space.

1. In your mind's eye, look at the person who rubbed you the wrong way.

2. Say to yourself 'I thank you for showing me this side of myself'. Even if you don't believe it for a nano-second, do it anyway.

3. Take a deep breath through the nose, then exhale through the mouth.

4. Ask yourself 'Do I really need to give the person a piece of my mind, or do I have better things to do with my energy'?

After only a few times of doing this, something amazing happens, that hot button you had inside you cools down, or becomes like a pin head (much harder to put a finger on). If this hot button still feels pressed, there is some rigidity inside you. All you do then is mentally let go – say it and feel it. Sometimes I say out loud 'I let it go', and open my hands wide with all fingers splayed.

This does not mean the hot button goes away permanently, it means it won't be triggered by this type of situation so easily next time. What you can achieve is a great lessening of the hot button's effects to the point that if it does gets pressed again in future, you can observe the reaction in yourself rather than completely become the reaction.

3. Dealing with Unpleasant Feelings/Thoughts

The mundane aspects of life like shopping and housework can make a person cranky, especially if they deal with delays and it's taken up more of their day than they hoped or planned. Ego comes to roost dropping thoughts that entrench the cranky feelings. Once when I had a sinking feeling which I couldn't shake off, I started to say 'I love you' to it. The ego can't handle unconditional love, at all, as you are supposed to react badly in any way possible, so the feeling evaporated.

The following two exercises are gentle but firm with ego. Even if you think the feelings or thoughts have no business being there, it's more effective to accept and release them, than to question or deny them.

Exercise: Give thanks

This exercise will counter a negative thought that pops into your head, or a stream of negative thoughts. It also works for repetitive thoughts that keep returning.

1. Hold the thought(s) in your mind, like a freeze-frame.

2. Say 'I accept your truth and I thank you for worrying about me'.

3. Open your hands wide, palms up, as you release the thought. You can raise your hands up as if you are boosting it into the air.

4. Take a deep breath through the nose, and exhale through the mouth.

Exercise: Unconditional Love

To counter an unpleasant feeling that seems to have lodged in you.

1. In your mind's eye picture you facing yourself, but this other you looks untidy, forlorn and seems unsure. You can't help but feel sorry for it.

2. Say to this other you 'I do care how you feel and now I understand.'

3. Take a step closer and say ' I love you no matter what'.

4. Then say 'I accept you. I need you. We are together.'

If you are sincere as you do this technique, you will feel a release from the unpleasant feeling. If the feeling returns later, repeat the exercise.

Exercise: Mind Jingles

The ego mind tends to get hooked on clichés. For example, one morning I repeating the phrase 'Everything's going to be all right', knowing it's a very boring and overused cliché.

I knew my mind would latch on to it because it seems to have no trouble remembering something annoying or clichéd. So my mind did wrap itself around this phrase and I was able to block a lot of counter-productive thoughts.

4. Dealing with Fear When Facing a Challenge

I've had to grapple with crushing self doubt. But I know that if I let it swallow me, I will sabotage myself. If you have nervous tension or a fear like stage fright, you don't resist it but release it. What I don't like about ego is that when it comes to irrational fear, the amount that is felt is way out of proportion to the supposed threat.

The fear that comes when a person is under enormous pressure to perform at their best, can be paralysing and can bring about a person's undoing. An episode from a reality TV show I watched demonstrated this very well. The show was *The Voice* and I watched one of the Battle rounds. This is where two competitors sing a song together but alternate so that each voice can be compared.

The two young women competing with each other seemed to have a positive attitude all during the coaching right up to the night of the Battle round. Before they go on stage, there is a cut-away scene where each competitor talks about their attitude and state of mind, and how they are going to approach the contest and their nerves. One of the women suddenly about-faced on her neutral attitude and said she was going to 'psyche out' the other woman. In fact, she ended up psyching *herself* out.

It was funny to watch her as she would spin around on her heel and try to outdo the other. Instead she came across as forced and desperate and her performance was not as good as it could have been. Needless to say she lost that round to her competitor.

While I am not suggesting you are likely to want to psyche someone out who you perceive is your competition, I wanted to show how ego can seem to build you up, but if it does so by putting the other one down, then it will only back-fire.

Exercise: Are you worth it?

Do this exercise internally in your mind, right up to the moment when you are about to do the challenging thing you fear.

1.   Straighten your shoulders and back so you are not slouching.

2.   Slow your breathing by taking a few slow deep breaths.

3.   Invite the fear to express itself fully inside you mentally and emotionally to taste it so you know its flavour.

4.   Allow this fear to make you feel awful for those few seconds as it peaks. (Part of the strength of fear is when a person tries to deny, resist, or fight it.).

5.   Say to the feeling (when its peaking): 'I am sorry, but I can't afford you. You are too expensive.'

6.   Release the fear by allowing it to drain through your body as if you were full of holes like a strainer.

This works well because ego is always telling us we can't afford this or we cant afford that. Since it believes in lack, it will not argue back. Fear thrives on resistance and pulling back from it, so if you do the opposite by letting it be, it will drain away.

5. Facing Negativity from a Family Member

I discovered this technique when my pre-teen daughter was upset with me because I said no to something. She just would not take 'No' for an answer. So she tried to verbally bulldoze me. So much for parental authority, I thought. What usually happens is that both sides dig their heels in and the situation can get out of control and someone will lose their temper. Usually me, then as she got older, her.

Exercise: Dance with Me

Do this technique at the time the person is being negative to you. It works best if you do it at the early stages of the negativity, not so well after it has escalated. It's really like nipping it in the bud.

1. While the person is being negative, take both their hands in your hands.

2. Do a heel-toe, heel-toe tap with your foot, then side-skip four times – taking this person with you.

3. Stop and repeat for the other foot.

4. While the person keeps insisting, make them do a twirl, and repeat.

5. If the person asks 'What in blazes are you doing?' (or similar); reply 'I am happy to be home.'

6. Keep it up until the animosity has evaporated.

Other family members might see this so you make a circle and do the zorba. It only needs to go on for about five minutes but it has the effect of opening a window in your mind (and everyone else's) to let in some fresh air.

When the ego is being negative (either yours or the other person's), it fully expects that you will be the same. When you react in a completely opposite way, the negativity just evaporates. Remember, the ego can't handle absurdity so dancing when you are supposed to be upset will make it stop completely.

Exercise: Let Go

After having an argument with a family member, there is no constructive reason to emotionally detach from them and resort to ignoring them indefinitely. This just gives power to the ego and will hurt a friendship or a loving relationship and no ego is worth that. Do this when the negativity or upset is over, and the other person is no longer in your space. It can help to say it a few times with your eyes closed if your mind is stubborn.

1. Close your eyes and picture the person in your mind's eye.

2. Say to yourself: 'I take the [problem/issue with this person] and release it.'

3. Take a deep breath and say: 'I let my Higher self guide me to right action, at the right time, now, and in future.'

4. Be still and silent for one minute.

6. Releasing Bottled Anger

If someone tries to bait you into an argument, you may be able to avoid it but it can leave residual anger that should be released. Another time anger gets bottled is in a more formal setting when someone acts with a total lack of consideration and you are on the receiving end of it. You may not have recourse to set things straight with the person and you are forced to generalise the experience and not take it personally. Ego doesn't like this because as long as it hurts, it feels very personal. This can lead to hard feelings which swirl inside you.

I was in a situation at work where I felt someone was trying to sabotage me. I was working as a business process analyst for a new telecommunications carrier. I proposed a procedural change to address a potential backlog due to a sudden change in government policy.

I communicated this in a set of flow diagrams and emailed it among stakeholders. One person decided to reply to all and said that because there was a typo on one of the diagrams she wasn't going to read any further. She took this stance because her idea for a solution came before mine but was rushed, and she hadn't thought it through so it didn't seem like the one to go with as far as the stakeholders were concerned.

I had to force my ego to back down even though I wanted to run up to this person and make accusations. My FGS ego wanted to punch her in the mouth. Because I bottled my anger, my hands were trembling afterwards. I wanted to be rid of that feeling but had to wait till the end of the day when I got home. When I took the dog for his walk at our favourite park I did the following exercise.

Exercise: Release It

Try this in an open space like a park, or simply in the middle of a room. Do it a few times until you feel the anger leave you.

1. Stand and take a few deep breaths keeping your eyes closed.

2. Now think of and let yourself taste the anger. (Replay in your mind a part of the experience that triggered your anger, if necessary.)

3. Quickly ask the anger to move into your open hands.

4. Focus on the blob of anger in your hands and imagine you are gently pressing it smaller. (You may feel some tingling in your hands as you do this.)

5. Now cast your hands up and out in one big sweep and say 'GO!'.

You do feel relief almost instantly and the sharp edge of the anger fuzzes. Later you can do these letting go techniques if the feeling of anger or seething returns.

Exercise: Burn It

Jeni gave me her technique for those times when your ego stubbornly refuses to let go of something and it's giving you tension. It is also helpful if you feel yourself sliding into depression over something in your life that has no easy or ready answer and you feel overwhelmed by it.

1.   Get a piece of paper and write down the things that bother you in short sentences, phrases, or just a word - however it comes out. Even a stick drawing is fine.

2.   Rip up the paper and burn the pieces. You can tell yourself that only peace of mind will resolve the issue.

7. Feeling Dread before Facing off Someone

Living with ego is hard work because we have to make ourselves very clear to others to avoid misunderstandings. Even then there is no guarantee that our intentions are understood. This is even more the case in a multicultural society because everyone interprets information through the filter of their own biases and upbringing.

You may be confronted by a situation when you need to explain to someone that they've been wrong and they need to fix it. This is tricky because you are then dealing with two egos – yours and the other person's.

If you are dreading a reaction from someone because you are the bearer of bad news, so to speak, or you have no idea what their reaction will be and you are worried, these feelings are unsettling but there is a way to dissolve it.

Exercise: I'm With You

While doing something routine like taking a walk or washing the dishes, do the following exercise. You can say it out loud or in your mind. Do it a few times if you find it soothing:

1. Repeat slowly three to six times: 'Peace be still, be still, and be at peace'.

2. Then say 'Peace' at regular intervals, say three seconds apart for as long as you like.

3. At some point, say to yourself: 'Don't worry, we are together on this. We will face the music.'

4. Then say: 'I will catch you if you fall'.

5. Now imagine four firemen standing with a stretched-out life blanket ready to catch you.

6. Say 'I know I'll be alright.'

The use of different personal tenses, the 'we' and the 'I', is deliberate because fear usually involves more than one ego face. After repeating this exercise, you will notice that your feelings of dread dissipate and almost completely disappear. Now is a good time to gently tell yourself that the situation will turn out smoother than you think. Try to imagine a sense of relief as you think this. If the feeling of dread returns, repeat the exercise.

Exercise: Shedding Residues

I woke up one morning with dread dropped into me like an instant download. I decided 'That's it, I can't go on like this'. I chose three power words and repeated them for most of the morning. It's even more effective if you use simple images to match the power words:

1. Think of two images that bring you peace – usually simple images of nature like a shell or a leaf.

2. Bring them out like mental flash cards throughout the day.

3. If you prefer text to images, think of a word like 'peace' or 'ice-cream' and flash that in your mind at regular intervals like a pulse.

8. Slow Down the 'chatter box' Mind

These techniques work to slow down the chatter in your mind and make your mind stiller. Some people experience mind chatter as a single voice that won't shut up, while others experience it like a conversation in their head between two or more ego faces.

The intensity of the chatter box mind depends on the person's temperament. Some people have a chronic case of it, while others suffer it at certain times of the day. I believe it's a universal issue, we all deal with distracting thoughts and tendencies to slip into a day-dream that may start with the recall of a memory or a projection into the future.

Exercise: Clouds in the Sky

If you keep hopping on one train of thought to another, and you would like to get off, try this. It's the Buddhist technique of letting thoughts pass by like clouds in the sky. If you want to be gentle about shedding your thoughts, this works well:

1. For every thought(s), think of it as a cloud in the sky.
2. The sky is the canvass of your mind.
3. Watch the clouds come and go.

Exercise: Hot Potato

Often, thoughts happen so fast that the Clouds technique would make them whiz by, not a peaceful effect. As Jeni once observed of herself:

'They were fast, fleeting thoughts that whipped through my mind very quickly.'

When your thoughts are fast, try this:

1. Pretend your thoughts are hot potatoes that keep dropping into your hands.

2. Instantly drop every hot potato – one after the other.

Exercise: Postpone your thoughts

This technique works well if you suffer from insomnia caused by excessive thinking or worry. It's frustrating that we can have a hell of a day, be completely exhausted and ready for an early bed. Then once your head hits the pillow the tiredness you felt for most of the day suddenly switches into a buzzing, like you've had too much caffeine. This is when you are over-tired, or had too much stimulation from being on the go all day. As you lie in bed with eyes closed and everything's quiet, the brain seems to shift gears and starts to replay the day's events and draw conclusions. It's hard to stop.

1. To every thought, or stream of thoughts, say: 'I will think these thoughts later. I won't forget.' and release the thought.

2. Say it every time, and *only* to the thoughts that are keeping you awake.

The ego seems satisfied with this declaration and you will find thoughts slow to a trickle.

Exercise: Peace be Still

If it's more than just thoughts keeping you awake like feelings or tension in the face or body, try this exercise. You can use a visual backdrop if your mind stubbornly insists on recapping and replaying. It is inspired by a meditation CD that comes with Susan Shumsky's book *How to Hear the Voice of God*.

1. Picture in your mind's eye a very simple image, usually the texture or pattern of something like the skin of a fruit, the surface of water, or the bark of a tree.

2. In your mind's eye, zoom in closer on the colour and texture of the image.

3. Chant to yourself: 'Peace, be still. Be still and be at peace.' (repeat).

4. Stop the silent chanting when you feel it's keeping you awake and focus only on the image.

Focusing on the texture of a simple object is effective because it will bore your mind. It works best if you chant the words in slow motion as this forces the mind to slow down to a pace that will attract sleep.

9. Lifting Depressive, Flat, or Low States

Repeating power words will lift a shroud of lower emotions like flatness or irritability. Do them regularly and every time you remember and you'll notice results within days. You feel generally more balanced, even when not doing the power words, and a lot less monkey chatter. It also changes your default emotional and mental states to be more neutral or positive.

Exercise: Favourite Things

Chant positive words to yourself whenever you are doing an activity that might trigger irritability, for you it might be driving, for me it's housework and any kind of shopping. My favourite power words are [pick your own ones if you prefer]:

Peace...Harmony...Abundance...Love
(Say them slowly and pause between each word.)

Tips:

- If you don't have to think about what you are doing, then reflect on the meaning of each word (to you) as you say them in your mind.

- If you *do* need to think about what you are doing, and can't shift your conscious attention, say the word or words like a beat in the back of your mind.

- If you find you are rattling out the words fast because you feel rushed and distracted, don't worry, it still works. You do get faster results if you can pause and think about the word as you say it.

10. Muzzling the Inner Critic

Most people have an Inner Critic, that biggest party-pooper of them all. (It would have to be Freud's super ego.) Its flavour is sour, somber, serious and supercilious. This ego is the one that loves to wipe the smile off your face.

This ego likes the status quo, the comfort zone, it doesn't like new effort or challenge. It is totally terrified of making mistakes so it's the ego responsible for setting limits before the person even gets started. It dreads the prospect of failure - and I stress the prospect of failure. Have you noticed that the prospect of failure is far more scary than the actual experience of failure?

It's great to be conscientious but the downside is that you can beat yourself up terribly about mistakes. So it's vital to let go more and have faith in yourself. The wonderful thing about ego work is that you come to realise that the inner critic is just another ego face – a saboteur. The inner critic can use more than one voice. At times it sounds authoritarian and disapproving. At other times it sounds more like the whining pessimist. When your inner critic is discouraging you, and putting you down, do any or all of the following:

Exercise: Breath and Release

1. Stop what you are doing for a moment and make yourself sit with a better posture.

2. Take a deep breath and release the train of thought.

3. Don't go along with the next thought that's right behind it. Let each one roll by like a passing train, one after the other.

Exercise: Use Movement

Do something physical that you're good at for a few minutes. It might be a dance move, or a yoga exercise, lifting weights, or a sprint with the dog. The exercise will oxygenate your brain pushing out the oppressive thoughts.

Exercise: Tease your Inner Critic

We are creatures of habit and that includes the way we think. The ego watches for a type of thought, or pattern of thinking, then it pounces. Starving it of mental food seems the most effective way to disarm it. This works best for the inner critic ego. It expects a negative and self-defeating reaction, and without it, will quickly evaporate especially if your reaction is unexpected. This is when you can get eccentric and unpredictable – I mean inside your head of course. You can have fun taming this ego because it is the antithesis of fun.

The mind loves to rationalise and it doesn't cope at all with irrationality. It has nowhere to turn. Now this one is radical, and you would let your intuition choose the right moment when to apply it and what words to use. The best time is when this ego thinks it has you under its spell and that you are taking it seriously.

Face your inner critic ego (in your mind's eye) and ask it:

> **'Do I know you?'**
> *[in a gentle and polite but slightly officious way like you've been interrupted]*

Or,

> **'In what way are you qualified to say this?'**

The key is to be very polite. You could even get playful and say to the ego:

> **'Gee, you look funny. Have you had a look at yourself lately?'**

Suddenly you feel still inside. Observe as your ego is stunned that you're using the same tactics on it that it uses on you, but without the snarly manner that it has.

I can't emphasise enough that you must be jovial and forgiving. What happens next is enough to make you giggle. A tension just falls away and it feels like there's a stalemate inside you as ego sucks in its breath in horror and tries to recover. This is a good moment to find yourself in and the situation goes from self-smothering to funny and light. In fact you will taste freedom. If freedom had a flavour this is it.

The objective with ego work is to reduce the amount of time you spend in an ego state, and it's a worthy challenge. For me, with my over-sized ego, I would call it rocket science without the maths. But it is really worth the effort because it's free and it will free you. Your general health improves so much it will be startling. Nothing else will bring you permanent peace than the work on the ego. You become the captain of your own ship, the SS [*fill in your name*].

As for dedication and discipline, all you need is clear and strong intention. I too lose momentum now and then, but I remember that if I let myself do that I'll be back at square one. Since I'm so sick of that, I have a real spur to keep going and not let up. Now I have reached the stage where it takes much less effort. Something I never expected is that the things in my life I can't change and I never liked don't affect me nearly as much, barely at all in fact.

Chapter 7: Mentoring Your Ego

The shadow is the lesser-known dark side of our personality containing the primitive, negative human emotions and impulses. Jung's definition of shadow is different from Freud's id which he defined as a person's 'basic instinctive gratification'. Jung identified the shadow as the qualities we deny in ourselves because others have rejected them, or, are qualities judged by society to be unacceptable or inferior. Generally, they include traits like sexual lust, desire for power, personality quirks, and the anti-social qualities like greed, bitterness, jealousy, antipathy, and rage.

In spiritual psychology it can be thought of as a splinter of the ego that the ego itself has quarantined to take blame and be condemned to personal rejection. This means shadow is always simmering below the surface waiting for an opportunity to bust through the veneer of the conscious ego. The less it can show itself, and the deeper the denial and rejection by the conscious ego, the longer the shadow.

As a result, there is human potential that is never let out, and because it's denied expression, shadow becomes twisted by its sense of tragic betrayal. There is a story that Jung told his students: He once met a distinguished man who was a Quaker. This man was of such strong religious faith that he could not even believe for a moment that he had ever done anything wrong in his life.

'And do you know what happened to his children?' Jung asked his class. 'The son became a thief, and the daughter a prostitute. Because the father would not take on his shadow, his share in the imperfection of human nature, his children were compelled to live out the dark side which he had ignored.'

The 'Hidden Side of our Psychological Moon'

There is a modern Gnostic understanding of shadow derived from the *Gospel of St Thomas*. It is known as the 'hidden side of our psychological moon'. This is the face of the moon we never see because of its orbital pattern around earth. In our psyche, it is feelings and attitudes we are not consciously aware of because they've been concealed in our minds by denial. They are the parts of ourself that we hid because they were met with disapproval from others when we were young and still developing. Since we crave acceptance from others, any part of our character that was not liked or approved of had to be stuffed away.

In *The Gospel of Thomas*, Saying no. 70, Jesus speaks about the shadow and the getting of salvation through spiritual (psychological) introspection. He said:

'If you bring forth what is within you, what you
have will save you.
If you do not bring it forth, what you do not have
within you, will kill you.'[24]

In today's terms, what Jesus meant was that if you release
and heal the dark side, you will free yourself. If you don't, then
what you lack as a result of not redeeming it, will enslave you.
The shadow is most destructive, insidious and dangerous when
habitually repressed. When this happens, it shows itself in a
myriad of unpredictable psychological disturbances ranging
from neurosis to psychosis.

The most common way shadow appears is when we project
hidden aspects of ourselves that others bring out of us, back
onto them. This was identified by Freud's defense mechanism
known as 'projection' and is how most people deny their
shadow, and, unconsciously cast it onto others to avoid
confronting it in themselves. The projection of the shadow
happens not only within individuals but among groups,
communities, and entire countries, where an outsider or
enemy is created, then made a scapegoat and dehumanized.

Looking at this closer it could be said that it's not the
shadow alone that is evil. It's the conscious ego's decision to
enter into denial and imprison a splinter of itself, that changes
the shadow's nature into evil. This is why reclaiming some of
the dark side is the icing-on-the-cake part of ego work, but it's
also the most intimate and most difficult.

A way to detect your shadow is whenever you get a strong
reaction to a person or thing that seems way out of proportion,
or, you have no idea why you are having the reaction at all. It

could be a fearful reaction to something that is not actually a threat. I once had a reaction to a person I could not fully explain. I kept wanting to judge them harshly in my mind because they presented to me like someone who was at odds with my value system.

While I didn't want to make the time to go into it, I tried the next best thing. I confronted my ego with an absurdity it did not know how to handle. It worked well enough that it stopped bothering me about this person. What I did was accuse my ego of being jealous of this person, even though I didn't believe this was true. You may wonder how could I accuse myself of being jealous, then? Well, spiritual author Jill Shinn explains it perfectly in her book, *Remembering Who You Are*:

> 'There's a big difference between not believing something and having an emotional reaction to something you don't believe.'[25]

I was annoyed that my ego was trying to create tension inside me over this person. I wanted to feel neutral towards them because they were not central to my life. I chose jealousy because ego has a hard time admitting to that quality and I wanted to disarm it quickly. I also wanted to be sure it wasn't jealousy. What if my reaction to that person was due to a repressed part of me that still believed in a value system that I rejected?

Well it worked. My ego stopped force-feeding me commentary about this person. Now I'm able to consciously stop myself from being judgmental, even when it's very tempting. The main victory for me is that I no longer do it unconsciously. I become aware that I am doing it and I can make the choice to stop. This part of ego work takes time because it confronts self-denial.

Spiritual author, Dick Suthpen, in his book *Lighting the Light Within*, states 20 universal laws. One of these laws is 'The Law of Reflection'. This Law says that the traits you respond to in others, you recognize in yourself, both positive and negative. It has three primary manifestations:

- That which you admire in others, you recognize as existing within yourself;

- That which you resist and react to strongly in others is sure to be found within yourself, or is something which you are afraid exists within you; and,

- That which you resist in yourself, you will dislike in others.[26]

When you find yourself reacting to a fault in another person, this is an opportunity to dive into yourself and ask why am I bothered by it? Why am I so condemning of a person's actions that don't directly impact me? What is the hot button inside me that has little tolerance for this type of human fault?

Suppressed feelings like these should be brought to the surface and released. Since they come up behind us, we are not aware until we are consumed by them. They cloud our judgement and we end up deferring to our lower selves without even realising it. This is how we can sometimes lose sight of our behaviour and treat ourselves, and others, shabbily.

A movie I recommend for a sampling of the human personality types and their psychological moon, is the 1957 Henry Fonda classic film, *12 Angry Men*. A jury of 12 men have to decide the guilt or innocence of a young man charged with stabbing his father to death. When they retire to the jury room, eleven of the twelve men are already convinced of a guilty verdict. Yet one man intuitively feels that the evidence presented in court should be looked at more closely. The rest of the movie shows how he is able to demonstrate enough reasonable doubt that the other jury members, one by one, change their verdict to not guilty. Three of the most stubborn jurors have their own hard line attitude and it is fascinating to watch as their rigid beliefs start to crumble and their buried prejudices are brought to the surface.

It is known in psychology that part of the emotional healing process occurs when a person allows suppressed emotions to surface to find expression to make it possible to move on from them. Not everyone is comfortable with parading all the nuances of their dark feelings, so if you don't want to explore the feelings further, use some of the ego training and mentoring techniques to free yourself, or at least lighten your load.

One of the best all-round emotional pain healing techniques is to focus on opening your heart. To do this, try the following exercise:

Exercise: Opening the Heart

This exercise should be repeated at regular intervals for a lasting effect:

1. In a quiet time when you can be peacefully alone, focus on your heart.

2. Take a deep breath to fill your lungs and diaphragm then exhale slowly.

3. Tap into your state of mind or emotion you feel at this very moment.

4. Ask yourself 'How do I feel?' and wait for a few seconds.

5. Ask yourself 'Is anything bothering me?' and wait again.

6. Take a deep breath, through the nose, to fill your lungs from the bottom.

7. As you exhale through your mouth, squeeze out your breath slowly by gently contracting your abdomen muscles.

8. As you do this, imagine your heart has a front door and it flings wide open.

9. Take another deep breath, and see if you can detect a feeling from your heart. Whatever the feeling is, say to yourself: 'I accept all of you totally. Thank you for being here with me. I love you'.

10. Sit quietly for a few seconds, with eyes still closed, so the words can sink in.

Exercise: Releasing Emotional Pain

Use this exercise if you have to deal with unexpressed emotions over a major event in your life. It is something you can't seem to resolve in your mind or bring to a peaceful closure. It can take time to trust the universe again when you feel hard done by. Here is a mental cleansing technique that will help you erase or lift you out of any mental and emotional residue lingering from a life difficulty.

1. Write one sentence or a paragraph that captures the essence of what has disturbed your inner peace and won't go away.

2. Hold the paper in both hands and say:

   'I take this pain that has brought me fear.'
   [tear the paper in half].

3. Place the two pieces of paper together in your hand and say:

   'I cast it away, it is no longer here.'
   [tear the two pieces again].

4. Tear up the pieces even smaller and say:

   'I have returned to peace, my mind is clear'.

The next step is optional:

5. Place the pieces of paper in a ceramic bowl and light them with a match. As it burns up say:

   'I thank and release the pain, and now, move forward with my life.'

You may need to perform this ritual more than once. Don't be surprised if you feel strong feelings suddenly rise up inside you as you are about to start. It is a very good sign if this happens. This means that the deepest part of your psyche, that you may be out of touch with, is responding positively to your healing efforts. You can do this ritual as many times as you feel you may benefit from it.

Case Study – A Major Ego Challenge

When ego realises it no longer dominates your thinking as much, it may decide to react in a final stand. There may be a time and situation where you find yourself brimming with a strong emotion that seems to come out of nowhere. This emotion could be one that was repressed and long forgotten so it makes itself known in a last ditch effort to captivate your consciousness. Don't fear it but simply face it. This is what happened to me one day in the workplace.

As I mentioned earlier, situations arise in our life to test our mettle. These things never happen at a good time, after all, there is no good time for an upset, disappointment, let down, misfortune, or unfair treatment by others. I was in a work situation that tested how I handle unexpected turn of events that lead to a major disappointment.

I was working as a technical copywriter for a company who hired me for my experience and skills. It was a new role and there was a prospect that the contract could be extended. Yet the person I reported to (who hired me) made a point of ignoring me from day one. He gave give me one task to do that would only take, at the most, three days to complete.

I let him know I could take on more, but that didn't seem to make a difference and I had too much pride to grovel for it. I already felt a sinking feeling like I was condemning myself to a fate, so I couldn't muster enough presence of mind to at least try to chat with the guy. I confided to my agent and she spoke with him but he acted like everything was fine. I felt this was to discredit my version of events and to drive me a little crazy.

I straightaway knew this was going to be very difficult for me to handle at the emotional and mental levels. I can be overly sensitive and am introverted by nature. It doesn't take much for me to lose confidence around others and for that reason I knew I was in the deep end. I felt that an extroverted person would be able to find a way to get around this obstacle and not fall into a dejected heap. Already I was defining myself and setting limits on my ability to cope. In so doing, I was quietly aiding and abetting the situation.

I tried to get a perspective by imagining all the possible reasons he would be treating me this way. The only sane one I could come up with was that he was very protective of his work and did not like to delegate. For him, sharing his knowledge and delegating some of his work would undermine his ownership. Everyone knows that in the work place no one is irreplaceable. This is why so many work places are rife with people trying to protect their territory through the politics of undermining and exclusion.

One morning, I came to work in a quiet frame of mind. I didn't feel like talking to anyone. Not long after I sat down, this strongly awful (and unfamiliar) feeling came over me. It seemed to percolate up from the pit of my gut, through the heart area, and then lodge in my throat. I had to flee to the toilets. There I took a few deep breaths and drank some water.

For the rest of the day my head was pounding with negative thoughts, as I didn't have enough work to keep my mind fully occupied. All I could do was stop going along with the thoughts and silently repeat power word mantras all day. After the constant mantra chanting, another voice with helpful thoughts came through.

By the end of the day I was more tired than usual. After work I bought some food at the shopping centre and was driving home. I pulled up at an intersection and the car in front of me had an interesting registration plate. It was EGO.003. This struck me as being profound and I took it as a message.

That weekend I was still feeling the negativity and my DEF and IBW egos were trying to take over me by imposing a bad mood and lack of enthusiasm for everything. There were times when I had to fervently say some mantras to myself as the ego would start an ache in the pit of my stomach and a tightness in my throat. Normally I would let unpleasant thoughts rush in to explain away the bad feelings, but this time I refused. In fact, I was so outraged at my ego for wanting to increase my suffering, that as a result of this event, I transformed from a worrier to a warrior.

I realized something special was going on when I felt my ego percolate up inside me as a physical sensation. It was the first time I saw the ego as me, yet separate. It was a wonderful gift as I have never experienced it manifest first in the body. It has always instantly slipped into my mind first and I would lose all self awareness and do its bidding. I can only know this now because of how it happened. That's when I realized this bad experience was really an opportunity, not only to grow, but to release past pain and heal myself in the process.

Intuition told me this was an ego face that was deeply entrenched in me and had a lot of clout. It could also be like a team leader of my other ego faces. Since it was being brought out to the open, I realized it was an opportunity to work on it. At night with some time alone, I faced it in my mind's eye, picturing it as the same face as me.

It is the ego face that never offers constructive advice in a disappointing or testing situation but will always try to cast me as a victim. I think it was a strange pairing between my Inner Critic and IBW ego. I told 'me' that 'I love you' and talked about me in totally accepting ways even though I did not like this ego. This worked like magic but only when I was sincere.

For several days I stood on alert for this ego feeling, because by now I knew its flavor in my mind. Whenever I could detect it by word or feeling, I immediately gave it attention. I paused with what I was doing and told it 'I love you'. I told it we are stronger together than apart. (See the section 'Working with the Shadow' for some sample scripts.) What is interesting about ego work is that even if you are dealing with an ego that seems to be aggressive, it still responds to total acceptance. This proves that all ego faces are based on fear.

During this time I was watching some of the reruns of the original *Star Trek* series (with William Shatner as Captain Kirk). There is an episode that deals with the shadow side with insight and sensitivity. It is called 'The Enemy Within'. I recommend it if you want to study the shadow. Briefly, the story goes that Kirk becomes split into two of himself after a transporter accident. One of him is good and the other one is bad. There is an assumption that the good one lacks strength but at least it's credited with not having fear like the bad one has. It demonstrates how we are stronger and more whole when we are fully united with all aspects of our selves. I think the good part does not lack strength but that to continue to oppose the bad part only furthers the fight. It is about reclaiming something lost. The episode helped me to understand the emotional connection between the higher self (soul) and the lower self (ego).

Depression or stress can make a person wake up suddenly in the middle of the night or very early in the morning for no reason. This is how it was with me one morning when I suddenly woke up at 4:00 am. As I did, I immediately felt ego. It was a fear-based sinking feeling. It tasted like a milder version of dread. There was a build up to this because for weeks I noticed my mind was chattering more than usual. I will describe the steps I took and how I applied the various techniques already discussed. I think this event was a wake up call - that I needed to apply more of what I was learning not just read about it.

As I lay in bed with the feeling swirling in my mind, in my chest and solar plexus areas, it served up defensive negative thoughts. At that moment, I had a startling realisation. For the first time in my life, I was able to observe in myself a line of thinking that I always followed. It starts with an observation based on my subjective opinion, and is usually negative or has me resigning myself to some fate I'd rather not have. Then I start to spread that sentiment to another aspect of my life as if

I am having a reality check, when in fact the opposite is true. As I realised this, I said to myself:

'I am witnessing this thought, but I am not that thought. I am consciously observing it.'

Then I said:

'I see this thought but I am not that thought.'

I knew that if I didn't do something constructive, the inevitable would happen. It would cascade again making me irritable and prone to arguing with my husband later in the morning. For the first time I saw the pattern in me. Not in my life, in me! I felt like someone had handed me the winning lottery ticket.

Despite my heavy state, I was able to think clearly enough to do the following mantra (furiously). I thought it would not work because at first I was saying it in my mind in a panicked voice. But I stuck with it despite my lack of smoothness. I think an hour later I started to feel a shift, and my thoughts changed to more peaceful and helpful ones. The mantra I used to rescue myself, and kept repeating non-stop, was the one from Elizabeth Clare Prophet:

I am invincibly protected against any imperfect suggestion.[27]
(to help with bad atmosphere and destructive thoughts)

I then imagined me looking at myself in the mirror. Yep, as I suspected it was my mother lode ego, the one that gives me the most unhappiness. It is the one called DEF (defensive ego). It makes me react to disagreements in a manner that alienates people and makes the situation worse. I realised I had to stop blaming myself and have more faith in me and others. I had to stop attacking people in my mind, and at the same time, coming down on myself. That is how DEF operates, it is two headed.

I faced myself and said to me (DEF):

> 'I want you to know that you are a part of me. I embrace you, I love you, you are not alone, we are stronger together than apart. I know you are being wronged but reacting the way you do has only hurt you, yet again. There is nothing wrong with you. I am so sorry. You have tried so hard with no appreciation for what you do. I see now. I understand now. I need you and I love you.'

In the next section 'Working with the Shadow', I explain why you talk this way to ego. Next, I repeated the first Prophet mantra again. Then following my intuition, I turned to my ego and did the face-off with love as described above, again. At around 6:00 am, I changed the mantra to another one of Prophet's:

> I am the presence of Divine Love at all times.
> *(to stop interference of the outer mind)*

I thought it now safe to say this one instead as DEF ego had loosened its strangle-hold on me. I realised that this gap could provide an opening for another ego to enter through my thoughts, so in the early hours of the morning while lying in bed, I said the following conjuration which came to me through my higher self. I said it several times in multiples of three:

Circle of Protection

I am surrounded by the divine white light
of my eternal being
It nourishes and protects me and gives me strength
All negative energies directed at me are bounced off
And returned to their sender.
It is so. It is done.

I felt this all came about because I was making progress with my ego work. The Gnostics say that as you move higher, there is an attempt by ego to subterfuge. I felt by this stage that I was over the worst of it. Even though the experience was painful mentally and emotionally, there was most certainly a chance to reconnect with the shadow part of myself. I was glad I had this opportunity. It sounds like I am glad for a bad experience, but when you come out of it far better than when you went in, there is no going back. It's like the difference between never knowing there is better, to suddenly knowing and living this better way.

I personally found that if I gave into ego's delaying tactics and didn't continue with the ego work, the pain of not continuing was greater than the effort I was making with it. This is obvious if you see yourself repeating old patterns in your life, and fall for the same fear tactics the ego cooks up. Feelings of frustration set in and the empty search for a scapegoat can lead to depression, or, something gives. As Jerry Hirschfield aptly puts it: 'At some point we reach another place of surrender. We become sick and tired of being sick and tired.'

Working with the Shadow

Shadow, when faced, is like a cowering child in the corner full of defensiveness. It fears the light and your rejection. So you need to tell it that it simply made a mistake. It is forgiven. I have applied this approach to myself and I can say it is POWERFUL and it works – even if you are simply dealing with your strong negative reaction to someone else's wrong-doing.

When I had that work place challenge, my ego was busting to take charge. Since I was swamped with ego feelings, I took the opportunity to get really familiar with their flavour. It was during that time that I named my ego faces. When the peak of the experience had passed, I was sensitised and was able to notice every nuance that I felt from ego.

It's a good idea to be attentive, not on the look-out, but more like your radar is switched on picking up the slightest movement. When you feel the smallest stirring from ego like a twinge of an unpleasant feeling or a random unhappy thought, instantly drop everything and in your mind's eye turn to yourself. Ego loves to feel important and you will have its complete attention when you can do it like this.

If you find an avenue or situation in your life when it would be the perfect opportunity to work with your shadow, there is a sensitive spiritual psychological technique to face shadow and coax it out into the light. I call it the Face-Off With Love technique. It's an announcement or speech you make to shadow that lets it know you are aware of it, and most importantly, that you care.

Use the following scripts as a guide to develop your own, or just use them yourself on any heavy or deep-seated ego feelings that are draining your energy:

Exercise: Face-Off with Love [Script 1]

'I know you are here and I am sorry. Please don't be upset or afraid. I am always here. You are a part of me. I don't reject you. How could I? You are a part of me! Together we are stronger. You don't need to be alone. You are never alone. I am always with you, I love you. I do love you. I really do love you. I accept you the way you are. There is nothing wrong with you. I love you. I love you just the way you are.'

It does seem like I go on and on a bit, doesn't it. The reason I do this is that the over-talking helps with gathering sincerity which you don't have much of in the beginning. Pretty soon your feelings catch up and before you know it, you are actually feeling for your ego in a caring way; it is quite astounding.

You can get light-hearted and appreciative too, and this works for egos that hold you back. These are the egos that make you doubt easily, create indecision, or sadness.

Exercise: Face-Off with Love [Script 2]

'You work too hard. Now it's time to rest and have some fun. Have some fun with me. You deserve it. You should not have to work as hard as this with so little thanks. I am so sorry I didn't notice before. You are amazing. I am in awe of you. You shine in my eyes. I look at you and I am full of pride and love for you. What would I do without you. I love you'.

Yes the talk is sickly sweet but the point is it works! You will feel better in your head and your heart. Make up your own words that fit your own way of talking personally, by all means. You can also imagine giving yourself a big hug, while saying these things, or in conclusion.

When you first start using Face-off With Love, it may sound scripted and mechanical. That's fine, because if you do it a few times then sooner than you expect, you will find yourself doing it sincerely. The other key is to not hold preconceptions or set yourself a target or deadline. Don't feel compulsory about it either. Avoid the attitude that 'I should' or 'I must'.

If you don't feel willing, don't force yourself. Put it aside and wait until you get an urge. It has to be a labour of love or it's not worth your effort. Even though I repeat myself and say the same things over and over in different ways, ego can relate to this. Ego's trademark is the babbling inner voice or monkey chatter. So not only do you demonstrate you are no threat to it, but you are speaking its language.

You can start with anything in your life. Like at times we can't forgive others (or ourself) for their behaviour or selfishness. You don't want this to plague you and develop into a grudge. This is where it's important not to feed the negative situation. Much like good parenting, if you ignore the bad behaviour and reward the good behaviour, the child transforms. If the bad behaviour can't be tolerated or forgiven, as far as your ego is concerned, then the Face-Off with Love technique works because ego has taken this personally and wants to grind over it.

This technique of accepting and embracing your shadow will move mountains for you. It does not want to be rejected any further and fears that you will if you take up spiritual work. That's why it doesn't like change in general, and is suspicious of everything. If you regularly reassure it that you have no intention of harming it, and it is true, it will happily take the passenger seat in life for you. The result is that life becomes a whole lot easier and more fun, all round.

When there is nothing but unconditional love and total acceptance, the ego has no come back. It has nothing negative to latch onto. Each time you feel your ego creep up, either in your head or in your gut, stop what you are doing and internally appease it. Sometimes things are happening around you and there's no time to check-out so you can simply pause and say gently to yourself: 'It's okay, rest easy for now'.

When 'being in the now' becomes your default a lot of the time, you no longer instantly cave in to ego reactions. When ego reacts, it feels more like an early warning signal. Something you observe, not something you become unless you choose it. We are all held captive by our egos to some extent. Many secular philosophers agree. In the book, *Breaking the Spell*, Daniel Dennett writes:

> 'One of the best secrets of life: let yourself go. If you can approach the world's complexities, both its glories and its horrors, with an attitude of humble curiosity, acknowledging that however deeply you have seen, you have only just scratched the

surface, you will find worlds within worlds, beauties you could not heretofore imagine, and your own mundane preoccupations will shrink to proper size...or if you can stay centered, and engaged, you will find the hard choices easier, the right words will come to you when you need them.'[28]

What I like is that it implies a choice – we can develop our higher self (soul) or remain trapped in our lower self (ego). That much is true.

If you are game, there is a way to bring shadow out into the open that I discovered by accident. You may not be willing to wait until a suitable situation arises for you to work with shadow. Perhaps it's too long coming, or you would rather do it now than situationally. Here is how I stumbled upon it.

I was in dialogue with Jeni about ego work and it was around the time we were referring to it as a struggle and a battle. One evening I was reflecting on the day I had, when I started to feel frustrated that my negative feelings seemed to pop up at the slightest excuses. I blamed ego and told myself off inside my head. It wasn't abusive but it was very scolding. Well for the next two days I slumped into depression. Normally there would be a specific incident or two that would trigger the depression but there was nothing like that so I knew it was because I told off my ego and judged its worth only yesterday. I realised my ego had retaliated.

I took the time to observe the flavour of my feelings and the sensations in my body. I then used the Face-Off with Love technique on the depression. I felt very sincere while doing it because I realised what I had done. I even felt sorry and reflected on what it would feel like to be on the receiving end of the criticism I dished out to it.

How I was sure it was my shadow was because the depression was physical and emotional, but not mental. This was a clue because usually depression is all three. Knowing that ego's scapegoat is shadow, I could see that in my case on this occasion, depression was one of shadow's faces because I felt depleted and powerless but without the thoughts that normally go with it.

Only ego blames another, not the higher self. So what did it do? It promptly dumped the blame I dished out to it onto the splintered part of my ego. Shadow is already backed into a corner and has nowhere to turn, so in its distress, it flooded me with depression at the physical and emotional levels.

Understand that these techniques of working with shadow do not eliminate the shadow part of ego. What it does achieve, from my experience, is it prevents shadow from silently undermining your efforts with ego work. It also lets you get to know parts of yourself that were alienated from your conscious awareness.

The Law of Attraction and Counter-intentions

The idea that thoughts are un-manifested reality is not a new one. In the late 19th century, the New Thought Movement began drawing its inspiration from the philosophy of Ralph Waldo Emerson, Mary Baker Eddy, and others. The belief was that a higher power pervades all existence, and that individuals can create their own reality by using affirmations, meditation and prayer. Early New Thought groups emerged from a Christian Science background by the early 20th century.

Another self help pioneer was British philosophical writer, James Allen, who wrote *As a Man Thinketh* in 1902. Soon after, William Walker Atkinson, an attorney, publisher, and occultist, published his book in 1906 called *Thought Vibration – the law of attraction in the thought world*. Both books were the trail-blazers for the Law of Attraction (LOA) philosophy popular today.

While LOA leverages the power of positive thinking, many people got mixed or no results from applying it to manifest their goals. The missing piece of the puzzle is the silent workings of shadow. If it's not understood, a person's hidden psychology can create self-sabotage or silently undermine their efforts.

Joe Vitale is a thought leader of today and runs a miracles coaching program. He is one of the people who helped introduce the Law of Attraction to the public through the movie, *The Secret*. He branched out to address an important aspect that was overlooked and was causing many people to give up on their dreams of manifesting their goals. His idea is that goals will fail to materialise if we have hidden counter-intentions.

A counter-intention is an underlying feeling that runs counter to your intention. If there is an underlay of doubt or even the slightest bit of unease about your goal, this is enough to block it from happening. An example is, say a person wants to start a business and they have the motivation, but in the back of their mind, they worry that their people skills are not up to the challenge (counter-intention). They procrastinate, and the business idea never gets off the ground.

Often, counter intentions are irrational fears from social conditioning that stem from family or cultural up-bringing. Let's say that one day you are upbeat, feeling motivated and ready to take action on a new idea. The next day, you don't feel so charged up and you mistake that drop in energy as doubt. You think you are having a reality check because you remember a parent telling you when you were a child 'It's nice to dream but you have to be realistic.'

Working on ego, you come to know yourself more deeply and may discover your deep-seated counter-intentions. Once the universe sees you are consistently applying yourself in this area, you will find yourself in situations that bring out these hidden aspects of yourself. All you have to do is be self aware enough to observe them and use the situations.

I experienced a counter-intention with a goal I had that showed me there can be parts of yourself that don't agree with each other. It happened with me when I wanted to have a second child. I really wanted one very much, yet I could feel there was a part of me that didn't want another one (counter intention). It felt like a hesitation or a small doubt. To explain that conflicting feeling, I went on a mental trip that I was probably too old to have much of a chance of getting pregnant again. So the latter won out. I was only 95 percent wanting to have another child. You've got to be 100 percent.

If you do notice a counter-intention that you have towards a goal you've set, it's possible to bring it into the light and release it. The only way to be sure you don't have a counter-intention is if you are so driven by your goal that your determination makes you stubbornly resolute, prepared for anything, do what it takes, and nothing can stand in your way and this attitude stays consistent from day to day.

A goal that is prone to coming unstuck from a counter-intention is when you are not yet driven, but are at the desire stage. Desire is important but because it's often ego based, it's not enough on its own to succeed. So if you have any reason to suspect that there may be something that could hold you back at a critical moment, or undermine your confidence or resolve to follow through to the end, that is when you need to take the time out to discover what that counter-intention might be.

It's worthwhile to have some alone time to reflect on how you feel about the goal you set yourself to make sure all parts of your ego are in agreement. This may sound like trying to appease your ego but it's not. The reason you are trying to reach consensus with yourself is that counter-intentions often appear underhandedly and take you by surprise. You don't want to be in a situation where you are making all the right moves but at the last minute a hesitation or doubt appears inside you that you weren't aware of and didn't anticipate.

Joe Vitale reveals in his books and motivational tapes a Hawaiian healing prayer that erases mental blocks. It also lets you forgive yourself for having the counter-intention in the first place. I think this is powerful as there is no way for the ego to turn the counter intention against you. Imagine you are holding the counter intention in the palm of your hand. You say:

'I'm sorry	[*I regret feeling this way*]
Please forgive me	[*Please help me*]
Thank you	[*Gratitude*]
I love you.'	[*Affection*] [29]

Repeat this as many times as you feel it necessary to work.

For the really stubborn ones you'll have to repeat it over several days. I've tried it on myself when I was sinking into a mindset of losing confidence. I've had to say to myself 'so what if I can't logically see with my rational mind how I can succeed'. All I seem to look at are the possible set-backs and obstacles, but that is self limiting.

I must think and feel I am getting what I desire NOW. It doesn't matter how it's going to happen and how I'll get there. The Universe takes care of the big picture. All I have to do is sustain my belief and simply take the right action in the moment. It's only in the present moment that you have the power to do anything anyway. The only thing that can stop me is if my heart wasn't in it.

You might spend days bouncing back and forth between feeling positive and having doubts. If this frustrates you, try to make a metaphor of the dilemma. It will make it easier to deal with it in your mind.

Here is a good example: Imagine you get in your car to go and see a movie. You put your car in drive, but then you hesitate like you are about to change your mind, so you put it back into park. Then you think, no you should go, so you put it in drive again, but then you wonder are you really in the mood? So you put it back into park. The net effect is that you have wasted time and effort and achieved nothing. Don't sabotage yourself. Instead make a skit out of the dilemma so you can delete the whole syndrome in your mind like a movie file.

Your goals manifest in the physical world when they are fed by a matching and consistent motivation (vibration) that is buttressed by feelings and thoughts which stimulate the right action. This is why passionate and driven people get what they want.

Whenever you set a goal, refuse to speculate about your chances. If you let yourself worry at all, it will make you nervous, procrastinate, and prone to making mistakes. If this happens, your doubts are reinforced and this will undermine your confidence. So you can see that thoughts can make or break you.

When you are positive, where before you had a negative outlook, you change the way you see things and suddenly you see opportunities and perspectives that were invisible to you before. I've discovered that if you change your attitude and stick to it, you do in time change your reality for the better. It happens naturally, without planning, like an outflow.

You can attract a future experience because the future is fluid – still in the sea of quantum potential. The future you have in mind is one of the trunk lines (or branches) of possible future outcomes. If you want to fish this outcome out of the sea of potentiality you have to resonate with it by matching your thoughts, attitude, emotions and actions. You also behave as if you have arrived at that point. This future is just as possible as any other variation.

By having faith in the outcome you want, and believe this future already exists, you will cause it to come into material focus. But you still have to make the necessary efforts to get it done. The difference is that the effort will flow from you rather than have to be forced out by sweating it. Many people made the mistake that all they needed was right attitude and positive thinking.

The Law of Attraction could be summed up by the saying: 'Where your attention goes, your energy flows.' You attract what you concentrate upon most and you can attract to you only those qualities you already possess. So, if you want peace and harmony in your life, you must become those things first. This is why you don't need to change anything in your life because these things will change after you do.

The Bible refers to the Law of Attraction in Mark 11:24:

> 'Whatever you desire, when you pray, believe that you receive them and you shall have them. Ask and it shall be given you, seek and you shall find, knock, and it shall be opened unto you.'

The Power of Silence

In western culture we don't value silence, like quiet reflective times alone, silence without TV in the background, or moments with others when nothing is said. We are surrounded by noise and white noise, especially since the digital age. Ego doesn't like silence and if you pause and try to stop thinking for a few seconds, you can actually feel ego force-feeding you thoughts.

Our culture, being so outward oriented, makes people uncomfortable with silence in a social setting and a person will rush in to fill the void. Silence is the antidote to defensiveness, or motor mouth, which is such a quick-sand. People in positions of power in society will often use silence. Take the example of a job interview. At times the interviewer says nothing for a few seconds after the candidate answers a question.

They may be reflecting on their answer or they may be waiting to see if the candidate will try to fill the silence by over-talking. If they do, the candidate may come across as unsure of themselves which leads the interviewer to conclude they don't really have the skills or experience to do the job. A confident person will not feel the need to over-answer.

Of course the silence may be interpreted that the interviewer didn't get the full picture, so it may seem that elaborating may be necessary to get the point across. But let's look at it another way. When in an interview situation or something similar, ego can't wait to step in (without thinking) to make its point. It's possible to stop the knee-jerk reaction if you keep your self awareness up. Say you answered a question and it is met with silence. You can also become silent and that person will see you have nothing more to add, and this adds weight to your answer.

You may be asked a question that seems incomplete because they want to see what conclusions you will draw. They want to see if you have any biases or tendency to be negative towards a particular subject. In the case of incomplete questions, instead of jumping to answer what you think they are asking, you could say 'do you mean...?' in the context of the job requirements. They will then make themselves clearer. You can avoid the trap of becoming defensive or draw the wrong conclusions.

If someone gives you a brain dump and you don't know what you are supposed to address first you can say, 'I see' and wait. By that stage you will have allowed enough silence on your part to let your higher self take over. I will give you an example of why it is far better to use silence to let your higher self eclipse your ego, and get a far better result from the situation.

My eleven year old daughter went on a school camp. It was the first time she was away from home for more than two nights. On the second day of the 5-day camp she rang and made a fuss that she wanted to come home, saying she was not feeling well. When I said no, she tried to bull-doze me into complying with her wishes.

I almost lost my temper with her as we were talking at the same time and I've said many times to her - don't start talking until the other person has finished! I could have given in to my urge to yell 'stop repeating yourself', and then lost my temper. Since I am not a very authoritarian parent I find myself shouting at her sometimes, but at least I do set boundaries. So instead of reacting instantly the ego way, I stayed silent for a few seconds after she said the same thing for the tenth time.

Well in those few seconds of silence on my part, a fabulous idea popped into my head. I told her that if she came home early it would ruin a surprise I had in store for her. Well that was unexpected, and everyone likes surprises, so she instantly calmed down and the phone call ended quickly.

Because this idea just popped into my head and was very effective at dealing with the situation, I know it was my higher self. As it happened, I did have a surprise for her but I didn't know this until well after the conversation with her. The point is, it worked whether I had a surprise in store or not, because I needed to resolve the situation then, not when she came home.

There are times in life when you can be taken by surprise, if you are, then the power of silence gives you time to regroup in your mind, to assemble all the parts of you that can handle this type of situation. In taking a few seconds of silence before reacting, you can observe more and temper your reaction.

I tell myself, above all, don't be a motor mouth. The all too rare times I have used silence has produced powerful results. Just go quiet on someone and see how quickly they jump in to fill that silence. They might reveal a tit-bit that opens them up to you. Or it may be a case of they decide to help you after all, when up to that moment they were holding back.

I had an amazing experience that proves that even in silence people communicate. I attended a Brandon Bays workshop[30]. She is a fascinating lady who discovered a cellular memory healing technique. She applied it to herself and cured herself of malignant cancer after she was told she had only six months to live. I had the opportunity to attend one of the weekend workshops, as an observer, due to some marketing work I was doing for the local office.

There was an introductory session with the facilitator about the technique and then we were going to stop for morning tea. The facilitator said that in order to get best results from the cellular healing process for the emotions we were going to process next, everyone should be completely silent for the duration of the morning tea. There was to be no talking at all for the whole time, which was 20 minutes. This was to allow repressed emotions to percolate up to the surface (which they did by the way).

I went to the foyer and served myself some tea and cake. As I sipped and ate, I looked around the room. Everyone was in silence and moving around silently. We would look at each other, then look away. Unbelievably, rather than feeling cut off, I felt connected with everyone in that room. It was sublime that feeling of connection, and in a very palpable way too. I felt like everyone in the room was like me in some way, it's hard to describe. It was invincible. Contrast that with a noisy, non-stop talking, social occasion. I often feel cut off from people because their facades are in full swing. I will never forget that lesson at the Brandon Bays workshop.

Silence in a conversation will often reveal more about the other person. It's always smart to avoid answering instantly. I tell myself to pause for one or two seconds before I reply, because I've seen that when I give my higher self a chance, I express a much better answer. Sometimes the other person reads your silence that maybe you didn't hear them properly so they may rephrase their question or statement and in the process reveal more. I personally don't use the power of silence often enough. I have noticed with myself that my ego

Chapter 7 – Mentoring Your Ego

likes to answer questions instantly, or say its bit lightning fast, like I was on a quiz show.

Dealing with Other People's Egos

It's one thing to be able to tolerate your ego, quite another challenge to tolerate other people's egos. You may get to a stage when you are friends with your ego and you are both working together like partners, but you find that your feelings about other people's egos are the same as they were before you started ego work.

Everyone has to deal with being attacked or criticised at times. Why do people do this to others? It's because they are run by fear of losing control in some sense, and also some lack of self-worth. They attack and criticise to get themselves on the topside of the negative ego – so they lurch between self inflation to self-deflation.

Jealousy and self-loathing are particularly disabling. They put the person on a constant see-saw of emotions by making them compare themselves with others and compete with them in an effort to feel better. They are living in a self-made hell of either being better than someone or worse than someone. Many people are trapped in this syndrome and don't know how to get out of it. They don't realise that they can choose to be different. They don't have to be the pig-in-the-middle of the ego's influence.

It takes will power to make the choice to not bite someone's bait. If you do, then you are identifying with what is being said, as Don Miguel Ruiz points out in his book mentioned earlier. If

201

you let it bounce off you like a pillow, then this means you are not giving them any control or influence over your emotional state of mind. When the other person realises you are not reacting with anger too, their defences will come down as well.

This is an opportunity for them to feel their wrong-doing and make amends. Some people are so disturbed that saying nothing to them is the best response. They are not open to learning a better way so don't even waste your energy trying. Their meaningless attacks and criticism have no affect on you unless you let them. My mother used to say to me: 'Never reduce yourself to their level.'

It takes two to have a war or ego battle and you are not engaging in it. You are responding instead of reacting. Later, after you have held your ground, ego will try to slip into your mind a few observational comments like 'they actually think they can get away with this'. To learn to ignore taunts like this is a valuable tool, for me it wasn't easy. Ego will try to make you care what this person thinks and make you feel like you have been belittled or insulted. Don't fall for this line, it's only an illusion. When you pause on this notion it makes sense: if someone calls you a liar and you get angry at them, it does look like you are taking what they say seriously.

Marriage for many (myself included) can be a testing ground for your own weaknesses. With mine it's the flaw of temper. There can be a strange irony with relationships in that you get attracted to a person for certain qualities and outlook on life, then many years later, those very same qualities can form differences between you. This happens most often when one partner matures in another direction from the other.

I try to be tolerant most of the time but there have been moments when I let myself go with the knee jerk reaction that is totally subjective and ego-based. In this mind-set you can lose sight of the fact that the other person is not enjoying what they are doing at all, and is actually suffering too in a flailing kind of way. By getting back at them it only entrenches the problem and creates a mental groove, so it becomes even easier the next time to slip into this reaction. I can really appreciate how wars are so easily started and yet so hard to stop.

Have you noticed when you ever had an argument with someone and you lost your temper and said things you shouldn't have, that you felt drained afterwards? I know with me that most of that draining feeling is regret, knowing I could have handled it better. Yes there are selfish people in this world with relationships that are lopsided, but I believe the majority of relationships could be smoothed by tolerance, forgiveness and empathy. I said to a psychologist friend of mine about how I saw myself avoiding an argument with my husband:

> 'He does respond to kindness rather well but too often I forget to 'turn the other cheek' and fall for an ego response.'

She said:

> 'To me, this means that he would be willing to work on this with you.'

I said:

'Unfortunately at the conscious level he's not very interested. But subconsciously he reacts very well.'

In some marriages it's one partner who is hot headed and the other seems to be good at keeping their cool. One partner will not interrupt while the other yells, and then calmly says, 'Are you finished?' It really disarms the angry person as they expect their partner to match their anger, to justify theirs. But the person who keeps their cool gives their partner the gift of letting them see their ego just rode them like a pony. Dr Joshua Stone said:

> 'If one were to react, one would in a sense be catching the psychological disease of the other instead of setting the healthy example.'[31]

Our higher self has the wisdom to know that if ego reacts, it will make the situation worse. Ego thinks revenge is the best way to cope with an upset due to its fear of being ridiculed. Let go of that part of you that is touchy and over-sensitive, don't give it too much attention or it will create a victim mind-set. Here is a fitting description by spiritual author Neal Donald Walsch:

> 'Winning an argument is never the goal of a true spiritual master. Winning someone's heart is. The setting aside of one's integrity is not required to win someone's heart, but the setting aside of one's anger may be. It is possible to make a point without making an enemy. It is possible to be right without being righteous. Debating does not have to be debasing. ... If there is someone with whom you are disagreeing this day, would it not be

wonderful of you could disagree without being disagreeable?'[32]

In time you experience that being your higher self is much more fun and happier than living the ego way. Your peace of mind doesn't entirely depend on external events so that for example if someone is rude to you, it becomes possible to intercept your knee-jerk reaction to be rude too. Instead you might let it go or find yourself forgiving the person. It is our ego that feels insult not our higher self. Our higher self does not identify with the insult.

Chapter 8: Being Your Higher self

Over the ages, the higher self has been referred to in literature as the 'still small voice within'. Today, some spiritual seekers believe the Holy Spirit may actually be a reference to the higher self. However it is perceived, the higher self is always there but is concealed by our chattering mind.

When ego constantly tries to take you out of the present moment, you can use this annoying capacity to your advantage by being the gatekeeper of your thoughts. You accept some thoughts but reject others. When you develop this into a habit, you think less unconsciously and more consciously.

Recognise and Connect to your Higher Self

There is a clear difference between ego thoughts and the still small voice, which isn't usually a voice, but a feeling or a thought that is very clear and sure. Sometimes it seems to come out of nowhere or from the middle of you. The voice of the higher self is the same as you. It is you. But the higher self thoughts are loving, expansive, confident, kind and sensible.

There are no negative thoughts, criticism, scepticism, doubt, judgement or limitations.

There are times when you are naturally connected with your higher self; that's when you are doing something you love and are totally absorbed in it. This is known as fascination. It could be a book that's hard to put down, a favourite hobby, or passionate interest you enjoy so much you seem to be in another world.

It also happens when a person is in danger. At these times a person might hear their higher self as a soft voice inside them. Some people who avoided a fatal accident have recounted they heard a voice in their head say 'don't go in there', or, 'wait for the next plane'.

Apart from these peak moments in life, you are in touch with your higher self when you are consciously in the present moment (ie. your mind is not thinking about something in the past or the future). It is in the Now that your connection is clear. This is why ego always clamours for attention by taking you out of the present moment. For the most part it normally eclipses the higher self but for once you know what lies behind ego so you won't settle for less.

The higher self is easy to tell by the way it makes you feel - peaceful, confident and secure. It's positive and loving and will be discerning instead of judging. The difference is that discerning is observing something and understanding its context or 'why it is so'. Judging is merely weighing the worth of something to fit a bias or emotional attachment.

The voice of the higher self is always brief and to the point. Messages from the higher self are consistent, concise, and pack a lot of meaning into a few words. It encourages forgiveness and open-mindedness to look at a situation in a new light. The higher self specialises in win-win situations where you can 'have your cake and eat it too' and comes up with fabulous ideas that are original and ingenious.

Ego's feel is quite different. It has a pushy quality to it and uses a lot of words to say little. If you get so-called guidance from ego, it will tend to be reactionary and subjective rather than reflective and objective. It will take an us versus them posture, often creating an all-or-nothing way of thinking. It won't balance it's needs with those of others. It will be full of rationalisations if it lacks common sense.

When you reduce ego's dominance, you can tap into your intuition and higher self more often. There may be times when it's hard to tell if an idea was from the ego or your higher self. When something is sensed intuitively, like an inspiration or a hunch, the mind steps in to process it and that's when the ego can creep in. This is when the idea can become tainted by a judgement or a blind spot. Another way to tell if it's ego is if you get a bold or ambitious idea but then it gets squashed by another voice that says it can't be done but doesn't offer any suggestions or alternatives.

Communication from your higher self will never contain ultimatums. If you are still not sure, pause from what you are doing, take a deep breath and make your mind still for a few seconds. Now wait for a sense or feeling about the quality of the idea or message you just received. Don't be put off by the dictates of our society which ignores the timeless good sense of telling the value of something by its quality or the 'ring of truth'.

A good litmus test is to ask yourself 'Is the idea I have beneficial to me and others?' What I do know from my own experience and working on myself is that the ego does take up a large majority of your conscious time. This is why I am happy to make sense of things at an intuitive level, rather than always understanding them at the intellectual level.

The higher self, or your soul, is not some wispy entity that lacks the feel and solidity of a physical body. It is real. The most obvious and accessible way to witness this for yourself is when you are lying in bed at night and are just about to fall asleep. At that moment, have you sometimes felt a falling sensation? The sensation can be strong enough that your body jumps, and you jolt awake. It has the same physical feeling as if you slipped on a banana peel. The falling sensation is your astral body quickly slipping back inside your physical body when it realises you aren't properly asleep yet.

Connecting to your higher self is best cultivated slowly. You don't have to meditate every day, just 'Be in the Now' as much as you can. Think of and feel your heart's intelligence. For many people, following their heart may not be as straight-forward as it sounds. For a long time it was considered morally right to deny our heart's desire in favour of the rational mind. Conforming to society's expectations meant much more. People would say 'follow your head, not your heart' as though there was something foolish about making decisions based on love.

Meditation is one way to reach your higher self but it's difficult if you have a busy life. Many people feel like they are indulging themselves if they do. If you feel there's no time to meditate during the day, you can try when you're lying in bed at night before sleep. It's not the ideal time as you can fall asleep half way through. You can silently say power words or affirmations to still your mind to connect with your higher self that way. When you feel relaxed and at peace, your antenna is up ready to receive. Once you start connecting, you will get the hang of it. I get a signal like my index finger, or second finger, suddenly lifts and drops to make a tap sound.

Try the following short meditation to connect with your heart's intelligence. You will only have to do this a few times then your heart connection will occur as soon as you will it to:

Exercise: Connect to Your Heart Intelligence

1. Get into a comfortable position in a peaceful spot.

2. Close your eyes and take a deep breath.

3. Tell yourself to let go your daily concerns for the moment.

4. Once your mind is relaxed, breathe in deeply through the nose to fill your lungs and continue listening to your breathing as you breath out through the mouth.

5. Now breath normally and listen to, and feel, each breath for about 30 seconds. Feel your chest rise and fall and the air moving into your lungs.

6. While doing this, feel your heart with your feelings. If this is hard, try to picture it (in your mind's eye) as

an organ in the space behind your ribs. See it pumping, and try to feel your heart beat. You can touch your pulse on your wrist to get a sense of the rhythm.

7. Now focus your conscious attention (your mind) on your heart, be aware of it as a physical organ and as the seat of Love and Intelligence.

8. Pretend you are listening for a sound from your heart. You are waiting for it to speak.

Do this for up to a minute, or longer if you find this pleasant.

Directing your mental energy to your heart can have a powerful effect. Once I had a thought that started to make me feel uneasy. As soon as I imagined my heart the uneasy feeling fell away along with the thought. This was a pleasant surprise. I was amazed at how quickly and strongly this was felt. Try it. You'll get an immediate sense of how much more expansive the heart intelligence is than the brain's intelligence which is very localized. In fact, science has recently discovered that 60 percent of the heart's cells are neuron cells.

The higher self does not wait until you badly need guidance before it speaks to you. It is always there and will make contact during a normal routine day through strong or very clear and decisive urges or flashes of insight. An urge may come as an idea or a flash of a feeling that is very sure. You always have a choice as to whether to follow your urge or not, but I can say that if you let your mind process the urge for too long, it will talk you out of it.

The result is that you may find you missed an opportunity to take advantage of circumstances, or strike when the iron's hot. The urge to do something happens when it's optimal to do that thing, much like hitting the sweet spot on a tennis racket. You'll notice that not only does the ball sail more smoothly through the air, and further, but the vibration on the tennis racket has a pure resonance. If you follow that urge you will always hit the sweet spot – when your energy is good and you have a frame of mind that's going to deliver the best result.

At other times the higher self will motivate you in a manner like 'action speaks louder than words'. You start to do something automatically. When I was writing this book I juggled it with working on a technical writing project. One day I was about to commit my third day in a row to my technical writing. When I sat down in front of my computer, I felt a curious but distinct flatness towards the work. So I followed the feeling, and turned my attention to this book instead. I soon felt a deep sense of peace and satisfaction. I was not getting into a situation where my 'bread and butter' work was competing with my book, but that both could be done, if they are done in turn when the urge strikes. So I hit the sweet spot on both activities.

When you are consistent and sincere with your effort and desire to connect with your higher self more often, little surprises will come your way. They are always delightful and sublime. One night I attended a dinner at a kid-friendly family restaurant. At one point I tuned out of the conversation at my table, picked up a crayon, and drew a rose and a heart on the paper table cloth. I was feeling very relaxed. Later that night, as I lay in bed to fall asleep, I became aware that I was free of ego. It felt so natural so familiar. I was still completely me, but free. This is totally contrary to the myth that the ego is what makes you who you are. I felt I should be able to be in this state again, it felt that natural. It was so nice, different from how I normally feel but not strange.

I can't find the words to describe it properly, but I certainly didn't lose my identity. I was mentally elevated and I looked down and could recall what it's like to be saddled with ego, knowing it's a temporary state. I stayed in that mental plane for as long as my awareness let me. Later, and the next day, when I tried to recall that sensation in my mind, I could not. Then I realized it was supposed to show my natural state to give me a spur to keep going.

When you take up spiritual growth, you will receive help and inspiration similar to this. It always happens when you least expect it. Don't let your rational mind dismiss it as time goes by. It's ego that will try to muddle your memory of it and make you think you may have imagined it. Watch for this.

If you feel like you are progressing in fits and starts, despite your best attempts and sincerity, don't worry. It's not that your higher self is not around, it's more a question of you learning how to tune in. Think of your higher self as a radio station that never goes off air. Just be still for a few moments and listen to yourself.

By maintaining a connection to your Higher self for as long or as often as possible, you will slowly increase the higher emotions in your emotional spectrum. The emotion you will feel most strongly, and which will take your breath away at times, is Love - on which all the other higher emotions are based. As the higher emotions take up more of your conscious time, you become more inhospitable to the ego's primitive set of emotions.

What's So Great about 'Being in the Now'

Be still and know that I am God - Psalm 46:10

If there was one simple way to control your ego and be your higher self, it would have to be the power of 'being in the now', most of the time. Buddhist Zen Master, Thich Nhat Hanh, and author of books on mindful living, says that most of us in the West live mindlessly. Our conscious time is spent on dwelling on the past or planning for the future, even if it's only ten minutes from now. By doing this, we 'miss our appointment with life' because the only time we are actually alive is in the present moment. Instead, we live in a near-constant state of distraction. [33]

The only time we default to the now is when we are socially engaged with others. At these times we are usually conscious of our presence in company, paying attention to social cues, how we come across, and what others are saying. That's a lot to occupy your mind. When I interact with my child, family, or friends, I get completely wrapped up in the moment.

You don't have to rely on social settings to experience mindfulness. I used to make a point, whenever I remembered, to pause from what I was doing and tune into my five senses for a moment. What do I see now, what do I feel now, what do I smell now, what is touching my skin now? For some people this can seem a difficult thing to do at first. Jeni said to me during her early attempts: 'It was hard, and a lot of work. Does it ever get any easier? Or more fun for that matter?'

This is where attitude, desire and sincerity makes all the difference. It goes from being hard work, to feeling natural, like this is the way you were meant to be. It is as easy as you are sincere. I discovered this when I gave up trying because of the effort, and waited for my sincerity to catch up, if it would. It did.

When you start to cultivate being in the now, your mind may step up its chatter at times. Be careful not to assume it's all too hard. Mind chatter is worse at different times of the day anyway, and depends on the person. If you become critical of how you are going with it, this will only encourage your ego to build up resistance. That's the last thing you want to do as the ideal in spirituality, and nature, is the path of least resistance.

On those days when I feel my ego pecking at me – peck, peck – I chant to myself a string of power words. One time I did this, there was a word that kept joining in and that was 'transparency'. So I let it. I suggest you do the same if this happens. A new word that keeps jumping in may be a prompting from your higher self.

You may wonder at this point, 'If I am going to find internal resistance to ego work then how can it be worthwhile?' In the early days, I wondered if I would get sick of the effort and lose interest. I realized, that if this happened, then I would have lost my sincerity which means I really should stop. When I arrived at this conclusion, I felt much better and more relaxed about the whole thing.

Bringing yourself back to the Now has a certain rhythm to it. If you refuse the initial panic of your mind and its attempt to force-feed some babble, you can start to hear more superior thoughts in your mind. Feelings that are sublime and tinged with love emerge later. Pondering on the beautiful timeless things, makes the mind less buzzy. It's amazing how effective it is to picture in your mind's eye a memory of something that has qualities of beauty, grace, love, generosity and art, in any form or expression. It's actually easier to stay in the Now taking this approach than being a constant goal keeper for the ego's pot shots.

Meditation as a Tool to Still the Mind

There was a time when Zen masters said the most effective way to meditate is by reaching a thinkless state. This is not realistic as you can't switch off your brain like a toaster. It's more sensible to observe the thoughts like clouds in the sky, and drop the emotionally charged thoughts like hot potatoes.

On some days I'm so geared to go that I find myself rehearsing when I'm supposed to be stilling the mind. I remind myself that clearing your mind for five minutes doesn't equate to forgetting your priorities for the day. It's harder to meditate by yourself than with a group. If you choose to meditate alone because it's more convenient, you can try for short periods like up to five minutes.

The spiritual author, Sanaya Roman, who channels a being called Orin in her book *Spiritual Growth – Being Your Higher self,* has a selection of meditations that use visualization. I like them because they don't require you to do it perfectly or for very long. You modify it to suit you. If it suggests ten minutes you can reduce it to five minutes. But if you want a technique that's quick and simple, try the following exercise:

A Simple Meditation Exercise for Being in the Moment

1. Sit comfortably and close your eyes.

2. Be still and feel for any tension in your body, then mentally let go of it.

3. Listen to your breathing and feel the rhythm of your chest rising and falling.

4. Think about something that never fails to put a smile on your face.

5. Relive that thing, recall the pleasant feelings that come with it.

6. Use your five senses to re-experience it in your mind's eye – how it looks, smells, sounds, feels and tastes.

7. Savor those feelings as long as you like.

If you are a restless sort of person, then visualising a favourite thing with deep breathing will occupy your mind better.

Being in the Now seems so natural you wonder how we ever forgot this mental habit. Young children are usually in the Now naturally. But as adults we make the excuse that because we have responsibilities and burdens we can't help but always be ruminating about something.

I've experienced the following benefits from 'being in the now' more often:

- When you choose your thoughts, or which ones to go along with, you are no longer at the mercy of mood swings. You feel like the captain of your own ship.

- You no longer get hijacked by the mind's constant commentary and replays.

- You feel more alive, more alert, and you notice more.

- Over the course of the day you burn less energy.

- It's easy to refuse to worry. You realise you don't need to rehearse your next activity – that's like not trusting yourself.

- You know you'll always rise to the occasion when the time comes, unless your heart wasn't in it.

- You become brighter, in other words you lighten up, and become more open in outlook.

- You become outwardly more peaceful and this positively affects those around you.

- When you have to get something done, you do it better, faster and with fewer errors.

- As you feel lighter in your body, whenever you make physical effort it seems less hard work (unless you're dog tired).

Jeni remarked that when she was being her higher self it was easier for her to extend herself and be confident. You will find your life gets easier on all fronts. It doesn't mean problems magically disappear. It means the problems you do encounter are less petty, and you are far less thrown by the challenges they present. You are not devastated when events take a wrong course. If ego rules, daily life seems harder or more mundane. Everything seems to take more effort and it can come with a mind-set that's over-cautious, almost like not expecting things to go smoothly. Life can so easily turn into a struggle.

When the ego's will no longer eclipses your higher self, you experience a feeling of wholeness and inner balance. No longer is your state of mind dependent on the ups and downs of external situations and people around you. You are able to take a wide-angle view of your life. You know that if a hard day comes when something falls through or nothing goes right, that this does not represent your whole life. Soon you will notice more harmony in general, and smoother outcomes and dealings in life as you are more in the flow.

When you are in the present moment, you are attentive to what needs doing NOW. You are not postponing life. And the resistance to action that comes from worrying, looses its power. It becomes easier to take action outside your comfort zone. When you are 'in the moment' (not thinking, just being or doing) inspiration comes to you far more easily. It is in this mind-set that creativity thrives.

The habit of being in the now is not about getting it right all the time. It's better to start with small steps that are sincere than force yourself. It won't be long before you notice your self awareness improves and you can catch yourself when you're slipping into a thought-stream or daydream. This means you can release sooner, before the associated emotions take hold of you.

I still get side tracked by my thoughts if something presses my hot buttons, but I pick up on them much sooner and can steer myself away if I want. Spiritual author Jill Shinn in *Remembering Who You Are* says of living mindfully:

> 'When you are in the present moment the most mundane situations can take on an unexpected, almost magical quality.'

Using Mantras and Affirmations

Mantras and affirmations are powerful tools for taming the mind and cultivating a more resilient outlook. They seem to tune the mind and body like a musical instrument.

- A *mantra* is a vowel letter, or set of vowel sounds, or words, that are chanted in meditation, either silently or out loud.

- An *affirmation* is a positive statement in a sentence or short phrase, and is said in the present tense.

Word Mantras

Word mantras help you gain courage, peace, and the ability to control your thinking patterns. They can be repeated silently or out loud. It is a creative tool because you choose your own words that inspire good feelings. Ideally there should be no more than five words so they are easy to remember. You can chant the words singly or as a string of words.

You don't need to take mantras and affirmations out of someone else's book. It is very satisfying to come up with your own. The more you try, with intent and sincerity, the easier the words come. You can play with the rhythm of words too. The words I use most often are:

Peace...Harmony...Abundance...Gratitude...Love

Choose your own power word collection, the words that roll off your tongue (or mind's ear) easily and have a rhythm.

Vowel Mantras

Vowel mantras massage your chakras and are more effective when chanted out loud. Chakras are the energy meridians that are like the interface between the physical body and the light body. The chakras interact with the physical body through the endocrine and nervous systems.

Chanting the alphabet vowels (a, e, i, o and u) stimulate the corresponding chakra points in the body because sound has a vibration. Each chakra vibrates at a different frequency, from the lowest and slowest at the root chakra, to the highest and fastest at the crown chakra. The following vowel mantra list is from the Gnostics. Other spiritual teachings use seven of the major chakras (or energy centers) in the body with slightly different vowel arrangements.

Vowel mantras are chanted from the back of the throat rather than just projected from the mouth:

Gnostic Vowel Mantras

Lung Chakra: 'A' (as in 'far') aaaaaaaaa
Throat Chakra: 'E' (as in 'egg') eeeeeeee
Third Eye Chakra: 'I' (as in 'ink') iiiiiiiiiii

Heart Chakra: 'O' (as in 'or')   ooooooo
Solar Plexus Chakra: 'U' (as in 'tool')   uuuuuuu

You chant one of the vowels for five minutes before moving on to the next vowel. The Gnostics recommend you focus on one vowel only at a time for a chanting session of up to 20 minutes. If you consciously regulate your breathing while you chant, you will find after the exercise is finished, that your body feels toned or tuned in.

It improves your general health and is a very enjoyable alternative to standard meditation. The tones create a resonance in the body that is very soothing and leaves you with a silky feeling after a session of at least 20 minutes.

Most Effective Way to Chant Vowel Mantras

To ensure you get that silky tuned feeling in your body after chanting vowel mantras, here are the steps:

1. Sit comfortably upright in a chair with your spine and neck straight.

2. Before you start, take a few deep breaths to relax, and place hands on your lap.

3. Inhale through the nose until your lungs fill up (expand your belly to make it fuller).

4. Slowly start to exhale through your mouth while chanting the vowel out loud, until you run out of breath (but not to the point of wheezing).

5. Inhale through the nose again, and repeat.

If you've never done this before, it may feel like a bit of work at first, but that goes away after a few sessions as you get fitter. Do it at a comfortable pace.

Making your Vowel Chants Resonate

When you vocalise the vowel from your upper chest, as well as the back of the throat, you will notice a resonance in your voice. It's almost like a stereo effect, where the vowel sound you are making seems to have an underlay of a deeper tone.

If you have difficulty vocalising the vowel from the upper chest, you can develop this ability. Here is what to do:

1. Vocalise out loud the lowest note you can.

2. As you do it, notice how it sinks to the lowest point in your voice box.

3. Feel that low note resonating in the bottom of your voice box.

4. Now imagine you are letting it drop even lower (into the upper chest). To do this you need to relax your vocal muscles in the back of your throat a bit as you chant.

Affirmations

Affirmations are positive declarations. They are expressed in the present tense and often start with the words 'I am'. As you say an affirmation you open your mind and heart and allow yourself to believe it. When repeated with sincerity, they seep into the subconscious mind. This releases the potential to materialise the intent of the words in your life. When you come up with your own affirmations, remember they need to be said with intention and faith.

They must be stated in the positive, for example:

'I am no longer weak' – WON'T WORK
'I am stronger every day' – WILL WORK

The following affirmations work for a mind that's in a worried state. Repeat them in one sitting for as long as you need to feel the effect. Later you may need to top up, but that depends on the severity of the emotion or thought stream you are trying to release. They work even if you say it mechanically with your mind on something else, it's just that it works more slowly. The following affirmations are from Elizabeth Clare Prophet:

'I am invincibly protected against any imperfect suggestion.'
[For bad atmospheres or negative suggestions.]

'I am the presence of Divine Love at all times.'
[To shut out interference of the ego mind.]

'I am the Presence which nothing can disturb.'
[For staying calm and unaffected no matter what.]

'I command through the I Am Presence that this be governed harmoniously.' [34]
[For when irritated.]

There may be times when feelings or thoughts can be fast, unexpected and strong. It can help to repeat something simple, easy to remember and quick to say like:

'I am here, I am Now, I am one with God'.

If you are mentally tired at the end of the day and don't want to chant anything that has a rhythm that could keep you awake, a single word can be soothing. One of my favorites is the word 'restore' because it sounds soothing.

The idea of a Circle of Protection is an old one. The Gnostics use them and pagan religions of ancient times used 'conjurations' to protect their energy aura. Use the following circle of protection if you are going through a difficult time, and even feel like you are under attack.

The following conjuration came to me one night (from my higher self) as I lay in bed with insomnia, unable to relax over a difficult period in my life. It helped me deal with negative emotions and stress. Say it out loud, or silently, in multiples of three. It will close off your aura to outside influences and negative energy (including your own).

Circle of Protection
> I am surrounded by the divine white light
> of my eternal being
> It nourishes and protects me and gives me strength
> All negative energies directed at me are bounced off
> and returned to their sender.
> It is so. It is done.

As you say it, imagine you step inside a hula hoop of pure white light. The white ring of light rises until it forms a dome above your head. From inside this hula hoop of light, it looks like you are surrounded by an aura of white light that has no border. The power is amplified if you feel sincere and believe in it.

Getting Answers from your Higher Self

I once read that Heaven casts out an idea or inspiration. It reaches say five people. Two agonise over the idea but never get it off the ground. Another two start but never finish. The last one takes the idea and runs with it.

Inspiration comes from the higher self when you let go of straining to find a solution. Sometimes you can get a prompting from the higher self that feels like a newsreader just being handed a 'breaking news item' on a slip of paper. In order words, inspiration can came while doing something completely different.

You can be confident of these flashes of insight if they occur out of context of what you are doing at that moment. The more you cultivate your mind to be open to your higher self the more often you will receive inspiration from it.

The 20th century philosopher and writer, Joel Goldsmith, said:

> 'When we become still and go into the temple of our being for the answer to a question or the solution of a vital problem, it is better that we do not formulate some idea of our own, outline a plan, or let our wish in the matter father our thought. Rather we should still the thinking mind so far as possible and adopt a listening attitude.

It is not the personal sense of mind, or conscious mind, which is to supply the answer, nor is it the educated mind or the mind formed of our environment and experience, but the mind of God, the Reality of us, the creative Consciousness. And this is best heard when the senses and reasoning mind are silent.' [35]

When you refuse to forcefully or automatically think with your mind, and consciously stop to feel and focus on your heart instead, you are tuning into your higher self. Don't be thrown by feelings, urges or thoughts that take you by surprise. This is not the same as day-dreaming but more like sitting back to see where the buffalo roam. Relax your mind, don't be conscious of your thoughts but watch them as come into your mind. Observe them in a detached way.

Ego may intervene and start to question or doubt what you're doing, or place an unhelpful idea or suggestion in your mind. Just dismiss it. Ego is always coming from a position of lack, never abundance. It always likes you to be predictable and will try to set limits on what you can and can't do. That's why sometimes answers from your higher self will bypass the mind altogether and occur as right action, you suddenly start to do something or move in a certain direction.

Not everybody hears or feels contact with their higher self the same way. Yours may speak to you through inner knowing coupled with a warm feeling or sense of sureness. Some people hear it through thoughts, like me. Other people see visions or have an inner knowing. You can get both inner hearing and inner knowing. Whichever it is, it's always spontaneous but definite.

Watch for a communication in a variety of forms. Our higher self uses what we know and what's around us to get its message across anyway it can. The answer may come as a whisper through a song, or something you read and you get an intense moment as the words seem to jump off the page. It could be quirky, but above all and whatever it is, it will strike you as being more profound than usual.

When your higher self communicates to you in your dreams, the dream will have your environment and people in your life as a backdrop and something extra, or out of place, that makes you take notice. It's a clue that this is no ordinary dream. Go with the first understanding you have of the dream and recall the feelings you had during the dream.

At times, a profound dream's meaning may not occur to you straight away, it could even take weeks or months. Usually when your mind is off the subject, you may get a flash insight about another meaning in the dream because something you are doing, or perceiving just then, triggers a joining of the dots.

I had a dream that seemed to say I had a block inside me that was stalling my connection to my higher self. I had to try to intuit what that might be. It did take me months, I must admit, because it wasn't obvious to me. After opening my mind to inspiration by not forcing myself to come up with the answer today, I let go and waited and waited, and waited. I later got the feeling that the blockage could be to do with my inner thoughts in general. Too much compulsive and forced thinking can get in the way of hearing your small still voice.

A person may get a download after experiencing an unusual or beautiful event. Some of the Apollo Moon mission astronauts experienced bliss or ecstacy when they viewed the earth from their orbiter, or when they walked on the Moon's surface. Astronauts Edgar Mitchell and Jim Irwin spoke publicly about their experiences.[36] They felt such a profound feeling of peace and love, that it never left them even after their mission ended and they were back down to earth. Mitchell founded the Institute of Noetic Sciences to explore the link between the physical universe and the human mind.

No Job is too Small for Your Higher Self

You can tap into your higher self for an answer to a problem. It doesn't have to be a major problem. The following case studies are real life examples to demonstrate that if you hand control to your higher self, you will deliver.

Case Study 1 – Finding a Misplaced Object

I was having one of those mother-wife days when everyone wants a piece of you. What is it about being a wife and mother that family members relate to you like you are a multi-purpose assistant? On this day, I misplaced my spare car key and an amethyst crystal I recently bought. After looking *everywhere* for them, I was squirming inside. By that stage I was quite anxious and on the verge of becoming fixated. Even though I didn't need these items today, I wanted to find them soon, and not have to wait until I stumbled upon them days, weeks or even months later.

That night I prayed and concentrated with a loving feeling that I would find them tomorrow. I surrendered my concern (like laying down arms) and *let myself relax and believe* the items would be found. The next morning I vaguely recalled a dream I had that I found each thing separately the next day. I thought the dream was nice but I wish it would really happen. Well guess what, I did find them. The key was in an odd narrow pocket inside my travel backpack which I'd somehow overlooked when I emptied it out. I am usually very thorough about emptying out day bags. Then I found my crystal inside one of my shoes. It's possible that I absent-mindedly picked up the crystal to clear a table and then dropped it into the shoe when I was multi-tasking.

Case Study 2 – Finding a Lost Object

When I go shopping, I normally carry around enough cash for food and use the credit card for bigger purchases. One day at a supermarket checkout I reached for my ATM card only to find it wasn't in my wallet. For two seconds I froze in disbelief. I recovered so as to not waste the cashier's time and presented my credit card instead. I had no idea when, let alone where, I lost my ATM card.

It is a real pain in the neck to cancel and reissue a new card, so when I got back in my car I paused before turning on the ignition. I asked my higher self to give me an inspiration as to where my card could be. I was not optimistic as there is a difference between misplacing something at home, when it never left the front door, to misplacing something outside of home. So I left the shopping centre as there were no steps to retrace since I had only gone to the supermarket.

As I was leaving the car park, I suddenly got an image flash in my mind of a $100 note. It's not often that a cash transaction dispenses this denomination of note so I was able to remember I had one two days ago when I broke the $100 note to pay for some bakery items. This led me to recall that the day before that I had paid a grocer with my ATM card and asked for cash out. The cashier had given me a $100 note. I remember because I had thought 'Whoopee, a $100 note!' (a little joke to myself). So I turned the car around and went back to the shopping centre to that grocer and asked the manager. In suspense I waited as he pulled out a thick wad of credit cards from his drawer and amazingly mine was on top.

Case Study 3 – Rising to the Occasion

Another time I accessed my higher self was to rise to the occasion in a social situation. I attended an afternoon tea at a retirement village with my husband and the in-laws. My mother-in-law had a presentation to celebrate the launch of her memoir written by an oral historian. The moderator invited members of the family to make a speech about the grand matriarch, beginning with her children then to the grand-children. Then an in-law was asked. Gulp. I realized the chances of me being overlooked were slim. This was a worry as I had not prepared any speech. Next, the microphone was handed to *me* when I thought there should have been two ahead of me. Because there was no time for my ego to react, and certainly no time to get nervous, I was able to speak confidently and talk about her in an engaging way. This is not like me at all as I do get stage fright. After the ceremony two guests commented on how much they enjoyed my piece. I have my intuition to thank as I had been doing Susan Shumsky's *Self Authority* affirmation prior to arriving at the event. I think it opened the door for my higher self to take over.

Letting Go is Not the Same as Giving Up

As long as the nature of our being is driven to the outskirts of our awareness, the ego keeps God from working more fully in our lives. It instils a fear of surrender and makes us feel that to surrender means losing control. What prevents us from letting go, is our attachment to outcomes and a lack of trust.

Ego always wants situations and people to conform to its specific expectations. It doesn't like to take into account other points of view. When you release your attachment to a specific outcome and open your mind to more possibility, the outcome is usually better than what you had in mind. You no longer struggle against the things you can't change. You make the most of what you have, and don't dwell upon what you lack.

The Law of Resistance says that you let go of fear by facing the object of your fear again and again until you make the conscious choice to detach from it. This often happens to people when they become exasperated and appear to give up when in reality they are letting go. Their ego will insist they are giving up.

Buddha's teachings also include the Law of Conscious Detachment in which he said, 'It is your resistance to what is, that causes your suffering.' Out of acceptance comes the ability to enjoy all the positive aspects of life and have the negative aspects flow through you without affecting you deeply. This is the idea of transparency.

Pretending to let go of an attachment won't have the same effect. A person may be affected by something but refuse to admit it. Instead of letting go, they decide that the person or situation is not worth their while with thoughts like 'I couldn't care less' or 'stuff you'. This is not letting go of the attachment. This is a dummy spit which invites a victim mentality. Like attracts like. This means that what you resist, or strongly oppose, you draw to you and perpetuate its influence in your life. Resistance and revulsion or disgust are a form of attachment.

When you feel overwhelmed and unsure of how you are going to approach a situation or resolve an issue in your mind, these are the times to Let Go and Let God. The following poem captures the tendency we have to quickly lose trust and give up. It was written by the American poet Lauretta P. Burns in 1957. The wisdom is eternal:

Broken Dreams

As children bring their broken toys
   with tears for us to mend,
I brought my broken dreams to God,
   because He was my friend.
But then, instead of leaving Him,
   in peace, to work alone;
I hung around and tried to help,
   with ways that were my own.
At last, I snatched them back and cried,
   'How can you be so slow?'
'My child,' He said, 'What could I do?
   You never did let go.'

I see a profound message here since all people (particularly ones like me) have a tendency to do exactly what's described in the poem. We lack faith and patience, and lose trust too easily. When we let go, we will get the outcome or something better, something our imagination did not anticipate. It's happened this way for me over and over again. Neal Donald Walsch, author of *Conversations with God*, has said: 'Just when it looks like life is falling apart, it may be falling together for the first time.'

People will often lose trust and give up just when they are on the brink of a breakthrough. They don't realise when they are about to turn a corner and instead, run out of patience. Another irony with breakthroughs is that things can seem to be getting worse, not better, and this causes people to give up in despair. But it's a natural flow with chaos leading to order. For example, when you try to clean up a messy room there may be a point in the sorting process where everything gets even messier, but after a couple of critical steps are taken, things start to fall into place much like a domino effect.

I read one of Wayne Dyer's books and thought he was a motivational self-help guru but discovered he has quite a spiritual approach to his work. In his book, *The Power of Intention*, he talks about ego and how it gets in the way of intention. He suggests letting go of the self-important ego priorities like: the need to win every time; the need to be right; the need to have more, and the need to defend your reputation.

Jill Shinn in her book *Remembering Who You Are* describes how ego goes against the flow of life. She says that life is like a river with the flow going in one direction. When we swim against the flow everything becomes much harder. The saying 'five percent inspiration, 95 percent perspiration' captures this. She believes this is ego's way, not Spirit's way. The way of Spirit is to go with the flow and follow the path of least resistance.

The same goes for human relations. Letting go and forgiving people who have wronged you does not mean they get away with it. It may appear that way on the surface but the Law of Karma (cause and effect) will ensure that they don't. If I retaliated to someone's wrong-doing then it would certainly not end there. By forgiving, or at least letting go, you release yourself from those bonds. Then you can focus on something else and have not created some unfinished business.

If you are having anxious thoughts that are making you unsettled, repeat the following affirmation a few times: 'I now Let Go and Let God'.

When you can slip into this mindset life becomes a whole lot easier all round. You are detached but fully engaged in what you are doing in the moment without being grimly fixated on the outcome. You are centered in yourself and taking relaxed and calm action. You feel free from the emotional chains you have built up over the years. You are not carrying around a world of things on your shoulders that you can't control anyway. You feel light and liberated. You can afford to let go.

Why 'Turning the Other Cheek' Works

There is a well-known saying that comes from one of Jesus' parables, 'turning the other cheek', and that is 'love your enemies, it will drive them crazy'. That this is an idea still in use today must mean it has real practical value. It's true; it works so beautifully if you can muster the inner strength because of what it does for the situation and the person being negative.

When someone provokes another, there is an unconscious assumption that retaliation will take place and this serves to justify the provocation. But what if you responded with kindness and compassion instead? I've tried it myself, very rarely of course, because it is really difficult to intercept your reaction. It works because one of two things happen when you don't strike back at someone with equal force to get back at them or teach them a lesson for their wrong-doing.

Their reaction is surprise and stops them in their tracks. In so doing, it reveals their true nature – whether they are mistaken or dark inside. If mistaken, they will become disarmed and sheepish, even apologetic. They may suddenly drop their rudeness or defensiveness and become calm and revert to talking normally as if nothing happened. On the other hand, if they are dark inside, it will drive them crazy. When this happens the person has just come face to face with their shadow.

Amazingly, this works with your ego as well. No matter if there is a part of you that you are not comfortable with, or even dislike, alienating it through unacceptance or denigrating yourself will only give it more negative strength. I once made the mistake of declaring war on an ego one day and swore it off inside my head. Well the next day I got such a thwapping with a low depressive state that I realised it had actually fed off my hostility towards it.

I have a simple but powerful example of how this can work like magic in dealing with difficult people and unfriendly situations. Sometimes we can be in the unfortunate position of dealing with a person's dislike when it's not called for and you can't find a reason for it.

I was 12 years old and in my first year of high school. I had a Languages teacher who seemed to take a dislike to me. For no reason she would pick on me and speak to me in a harsher tone than anyone else. One day she singled me out to give me homework that was due the next day that no-one else was asked to do. I had to write an essay on Roman architecture. I dreaded the classes with her.

I was to have this teacher for one more year and I was not happy about it. Over the summer holidays I went back to my home country, Poland, and saw my relatives for the first time. We brought back souvenirs including a school case of Polish chocolate bars.

For some reason, and I don't know what possessed me, I decided that I would give my Languages teacher a bar of Polish chocolate. I don't recall if I had reasoned that maybe I could sweeten her up, but what I do remember is that after I gave her the chocolate bar her whole attitude towards me changed. It literally reversed.

She was so chuffed over this chocolate gift, that she treated me like the teacher's pet after that. She changed from being testy with me to a patient warmth. From then on she was kinder and approving in the way she communicated to me. She even acted like she was fond of me. That was my very first experience with the power of 'turning the other cheek'. I am not saying this would work so well in other instances, but it is well worth a try and you only have something to gain, and nothing to lose.

Turning the other cheek is a very profound and powerful weapon, beautiful and sublime. Yes, it is the hardest spiritual tactic to put into practice, boy do I know that, but it is well worth striving for. It works because one of two things happen when you don't retaliate:

a)   They stop what they're doing because they see you're not reacting in the expected way, and their conscience may step in and make them feel guilty. 'Why aren't you angry back at me' or 'why don't you retaliate?' they would ask themselves. Your lack of reaction has made their action seem more extreme and reprehensible. They realise they have missed the mark. They back down and never look at you the same way again.

b)   If they continue to hurt you, despite you turning the other cheek, then you know that person is damaged inside. Such a person will actually feel fear in the face of you. Fear of such a depth that is inexplicable to them and makes it all the more frightening. You have nothing to fear from them as your lack of negative reaction will give them nothing further to feed off. It may be tempting to *then* lash out at them because you sense their moment of weakness. I suggest you look at them in the eye instead. They will always look away first.

Now to an example when my daughter was eleven years old. Being an only child, I have indulged her so she's a bit too used to getting her own way. I decided to strengthen the boundaries and limits more. I said no and I meant no to something she wanted. Anyhow she got upset, and she has my temper too, so she got angry and made a swiping motion with her hand so her finger tips hit the end of my nose. I felt a moment of outrage but decided not to get angry back at her. Yes it took some willpower.

I thought this is not my daughter, she knows better than this behaviour. So I just looked at her and blinked and said nothing but looked a bit shocked. She saw that I wasn't reacting with anger too, so her anger seemed to slip off her like a cape.

I said to her at that point 'Are you back?' and 'Is it you? Are you back?'.

She looked at me straight in the eye, and in a breathless voice, said 'Yes'.

One of the things I love about children is that they are more open to spiritual concepts than adults. When my daughter was four, I told her about the ego and she listened like it was an everyday subject. What pleased me was that she seemed to know exactly what I meant when I asked her 'Are you back?' We haven't discussed it much since that age because I want her to be a child and if it took until I was middle-aged before I was mature enough to receive real wisdom then I'll wait for appropriate times to tell her more about the mysteries of life.

Chapter 9: Spiritual Discernment

I've always read that a person will find the answers they seek about spirituality when their soul becomes ready to receive it. It's not a society-based measure around points, status, winning or deserving, and other ego yardsticks. There is no penalty for being late or slow to learn. This is beyond faith-based religion. It is a matter of the heart, the heart opening, and a yearning that comes from inside you like a deep spring.

A spiritual journey can open in one's life when they weren't actually looking, when they least expect it. You may even find yourself thinking, 'Hey wait a minute; I do the wrong thing, I lose my temper, I have too many dislikes, how could I possibly be ready?' When it comes to spiritual readiness, this is an area that is more individual than anything you can imagine. For every single person's life is one way to finding God, and there are seven billion variations on this planet alone.

How to Tell if you are Ready for a Spiritual Quest

The way to tell is quite straightforward, yet individual. It can happen when the ordinary ego pleasures no longer satisfy you and you feel bored when you think about them. A sample of what may no longer get you excited are the following:

- Making lots of money (more than you need)
- The lure of fame and status
- The desire for prestige
- Boozy socialising and being seen
- Straining to be popular, or with the 'it' crowd
- Winning at games like spectator sports and war.

It could come as an inexplicable wave of love beaming from your heart that stops you in your tracks one day. It could be triggered when you see a beautiful aspect of nature, or a situation where people are being at their best and pulling together to help each other without expecting a payoff.

It doesn't sound like much but remember feelings are powerful. We know that from experiencing negative feelings. The higher feelings that come with an awakening are breathtaking and ecstatic. The triggers that propel a person on a spiritual quest are many and varied but here are some of the better-known ones:

- A feeling or sense of knowing that the complexity of life and the universe shows that consciousness exists, both individually and collectively.

- Fed up with playing the victim and of being a slave to moods, depression, sadness, anxiety attacks, chronic unhappiness, seeing repeating life patterns.

- A persistent curiosity about the meaning of life after feeling dissatisfied with mainstream religion.

- A consistent desire to understand the nature of love, and love better.

- A mysterious yearning that wells up inside you.

- Having gone through a near death experience (NDE), or even an out of body experience (OBE), or some other profound event that causes a person to take stock of reality.

- Experience of a revelation, often in dreams or insights, even premonitions.

- It could be wondering about death: do we just wink out into nothingness after we die?

The first self-help book I ever read, long before I started my spiritual journey, was *The Power of Your Subconscious Mind* by Joseph Murphy MD. In his book, he retells a spiritual fable. The story goes that a young man asked Socrates how he could get wisdom:

'Come with me', Socrates replied.

He took the young man to a river and shoved his head under the water. He held it there until the boy struggled for air, then he let him go. When the boy regained his composure, Socrates asked him,

'What did you want most when your head was under water?'

'Why I wanted air, of course!' the boy spluttered.

'When you want wisdom as much as you wanted air just then,' Socrates said, 'that is when you will get it.'

Of course there are other less drastic indications. You may be interested in the mysteries of life and ancient wisdoms. You may come across a person's story of their near brush with death involving a near death experience and this fires your curiosity about the afterlife.

Joel Goldsmith, American spiritual author, healer, and mystic who founded The Infinite Way movement, has said:

'Our understanding of spiritual life unfolds in proportion to our receptivity to Truth, not praying up to God, but letting God unfold and reveal itself to us.' [37]

Jiddu Krishnamurti, regarded as one of the greatest thinkers and religious teachers of all time has said:

'Truth can come to you only when your mind and heart are simple, clear, and there is love in your heart, not if your heart is filled with the things of the mind....It is advisable to go directly to the source, the teachings themselves, and not through any authority.' [38]

The Bible seems to agree with the Buddhist saying that truth comes to you when you are ready. In 1 Chronicles 28:9, it says:

> 'The Lord searches all hearts and understands all the imaginations of the thoughts.'

Some people do find themselves on a spiritual path after suffering or a loss. It's not that people need a crutch in life and lunge towards God out of desperation. I think people get tired of being the victim and something gives inside them. They ask themselves why is this happening to me? At that moment they may become aware of a higher consciousness. This is how good can come from bad, opportunity from loss, and terrible adversity can throw a person back on themselves to force them to wake up to the fact that there is more to life.

The age old saying 'every cloud has a silver lining' captures this. Suffering does have a strange silver lining to it if you let go and consciously decide, 'I am more than this suffering. It will not consume me.' It is an act of defiance and rebellion for the right reasons. It is said that God only allows you as much as you can bear and then something gives.

How I found myself on a spiritual journey, despite no interest when I was young, is a point that many people come to, but even then there is a choice. You can see clues and choose to rationalise them away and get on with the grind of daily life. Even the experience of a great loss does not always bring a person to a point of questioning the meaning of life. Near-death experiences have changed many people's lives, but not everyone who has experienced them.

An acquaintance of mine had an experience that could have potentially awakened her but it didn't. She had contracted septicaemia (viral blood poisoning), was in extreme pain in hospital and almost died. When she told me about it one hot summer day at the beach, her arms were covered in goose-bumps. She said that at one stage when she was unconscious, she went through a very vivid replay of her life then paused in front of an old wooden door. She wondered what was beyond the door and that is when the experience ended for her.

I have never experienced serious illness apart from the mumps as a kid, but I did have a taste of what it is to know great loss - yet that was not the trigger point for me either. I had a late miscarriage. It was traumatic but it did not awaken me - yet. It wasn't until five years later, after I attended that Gnostic lecture that I finally knocked on the door and it opened. So tragedy, serious illness, or suffering, does not always directly lead a person to become spiritual. There has to be a readiness.

Jerry Hirschfield explains why we were meant to take an active role in our spiritual growth and not passively follow a leader:

> 'The very nature of God means He places no restrictions on us as to how to reach him. He knows that our path to Him must be one of increasing freedom and learning to take responsibility for our own progress rather than depend on [being lead] or being restricted by other interpretations imposed on us by other ego-bound individuals who are just like us.' [39]

Even if you start to look into spirituality but change your mind, or drop the ball as I did several times, there is a stage in spiritual growth when there is no turning back. This is after you experience positive effects from practicing spiritual tools like meditation, being in the now, ego work, and mantras to open the chakras. The change in you is no longer subtle and you realise you want more. It's like, once you thought the only wine is vinegar then you discover the finest wines produced in the world.

Remember Jesus' words in John 18:37: 'Everyone who is of the truth hears my voice.'

Let that be your guide amongst all the voices preaching about spirituality. It's a safe-guard because it means your understanding will be guided by the unseen hand and you are not likely to fall for a cult leader.

You come to the knowledge for the right reasons, in the right way, without falling under the influence of anyone's distortion of the truth. You learn things through your own discovery and self-help. The truth unwraps itself according to your readiness and the events in your life which trigger experiences of the truth. So it's nothing to do with a person being better than someone else, or having reached a state of perfect enlightenment, or having qualifications in theological subjects. It is all about readiness. Are you ready?

Discerning Genuine Spiritual Sources

When Jeni and I started to go to school on each other, it wasn't long before our comparing of notes had us come up with an idea of how to be discerning. We would toss ideas around and find some ideas that appeared in more than one place. After this, we decided on what we called the 'three source validation rule'. If the same idea was found in three unrelated sources, then the idea must be a truth. I found that I was more willing to delve into topics and sources that I would not have trusted in the past because I didn't have the confidence that I could tell truth from dogma.

For example, there was a time when I thought the famous American psychic, Edgar Cayce, was just a performer, someone who mesmerised people into believing in the occult. I formed this opinion of him without having read any of his works or looking up his history. This is how wilful ignorance works, you slam something without actually checking it properly first. One day, I made the effort to read one of his books and was surprised to discover he was not a charlatan after all. He had a fascinating take on the meaning of sin. His definition of sin made a lot more sense to me because it assumes we are consciously aware of our will and the power of choice. He said:

> 'When we turn our backs on our awareness of
> oneness and take our physical being, our existence
> in the material world, as the prime reality, we miss
> the mark....When we insist that our egos be the
> principle rulers of our lives, we miss the mark.' [40]

Edgar Cayce's interpretation makes sense. We sinned by missing the mark and going with ego. In spirituality, there is error rather than sin. The only absolute law resulting from error is 'cause and effect' known as Karma. It is also known as 'what goes around, comes around', noted in the Bible as 'what you sow, you shall reap'.

There is no need for rules because if you do something wrong it will come back to you one way or another. Jesus said that if we follow just two great commandments, that contain the whole law of God, that is all we need to live a peaceful and loving life. The commandments Jesus spoke of are:

1. Thou shalt love the Lord thy God with thy whole heart, and with thy whole soul, and with thy whole mind, and with thy whole strength;

2. Thou shalt love thy neighbour as thyself.[41]

The doubt many people feel about spirituality is understandable when you look at how many practitioners, whether in organisations or operating individually, are messing with the truth and using it to gain guru status. It's a shame, as they give spirituality a bad name and put people right back where they started by giving them yet another leader to follow, yet another restricted faith to obey. The ability to be discerning about teachers and their messages is a vital quality to have when starting a spiritual quest.

It is true that vulnerable people lack the ability to discern and are too fearful to think for themselves so they are the ones who become victims of cults. But they should realize that being alive involves personal responsibility. There are snake oil salesmen in every industry and ultimately we are, or should be, responsible for ourselves. If a cult exists then the responsibility lies not only with the leader but the people who make the choice to be willing followers because they refuse to think for themselves. There is much less excuse for victims of cults today than there was in the past because today we have much more access to information.

So how can you tell who to trust when searching about spirituality or finding a group or faith to follow? There is one gauge that is reliable. Everyone has an inbuilt radar - the bullshit detector, whatever you want to call it. It's a latent ability that we all have that we can tap into and do quite naturally at times without realizing it.

You can become conscious of it when you observe your mental, emotional and physical reactions. Basically, it's your intuition or gut feeling. It can be an impression that is felt as a passing thought or a feeling sense. Remember that saying, 'It has the ring of truth to it'? It's not used much these days. From an early age we are encouraged to not always trust our feelings. Our cultural reinforcements of ego, and the idea that the rational mind is a superior gauge on reality, tends to dismiss intuition.

It's important to be observant when testing the waters with a spiritual organisation. When spirituality is externalised, it falls into a structure with a hierarchy of one sort or another. This type of environment is conducive to the ego taking over. The teaching may have a spin or a bias from the master or leader, but you can still learn something from them without co-opting them into your life.

Barbara Whitfield offers this advice about discerning cult-like spirituality:

> 'When I see someone pushing an exclusive, restrictive system, I become cautious. Spiritual awakenings are universal, include everyone and

exclude no one. They include all beliefs, are anti-nothing, require no allegiance and embrace all.'⁴²

I have the Gnostics to thank for introducing me to the basics about ego. Their teachings also referred to Buddhist wisdom, and from that I learned the practical value of self-awareness and being in the now. Because I suffered with low confidence and negative thinking, it became obvious that working on my ego was essential for me.

If you dare to study with what might be a cult, ask yourself: is the message positive, constructive and helpful, even loving? If there is any kind of separation or duality, judgment about others, or an all-or-nothing approach, or claims to exclusivity like our way is the only way, then run for the hills. This is especially true if the cult preaches any sort of doomsday or apocalyptic message.

When I went to that first Gnostic lecture, I decided I had nothing to lose except one hour of my time. As I listened, I became struck by what they were saying and how they were saying it – simply and without any zeal. It seemed to make a lot of sense, I could not ignore or rationalise it away. Despite some questionable ideas that were presented in later lectures, I kept returning for a while because I recognized some truth. I was using spiritual discernment.

Unless you can find out first-hand about a spiritual group through a friend, you can make enquiries before attending them. If they have a website look at their About Us page (or similar) to see who they are. How do they financially support themselves - books, products, workshops, courses, donations? On what body of knowledge do they base their teachings?

The quality and voice of a website, and the way of their words, can reveal their sincerity. Are they matter-of-fact, or are there some strong words that seem to indicate they are taking sides on an issue. As a spiritually-minded acquaintance once said to me, 'Use your God-given intellectual faculties to discern what is fact or fiction'.

Using the internet search engines like Google, add the word 'reviews' after their name to see what experiences people have had with them. This is quite a reliable method of detection because when you search a subject on the internet you get a variety of sources in the search results page. The sources vary from official and professional to personal and questionable. For example, you may spot a university or educational organisation; a corporation or a small business; an interest group, fraternity, or forum; a personal or club website. The biases up front and easy to discern, unlike traditional media.

This means the slant on a subject can be gauged by the identity of the author. If there is little to no information in their About Us page as to who they are, have a look at the copyright information at the bottom of the page. At times, what looks to be an independent website is really a subsidiary. An up-front source will usually state, in the About Us page, how they got started and who they are, and who makes up the group. Unfortunately many websites use the About Us page (or similar name) to put a mission statement. In that case, look at their website overall, what do they offer, who sponsors them?

If you find a spiritual group and decide to take the plunge, use your gift of discernment to sift out the wheat from the chaff. There are charlatans out there who manipulate the truth to benefit themselves. Many people think they are representative of spirituality as a whole, but they are not. If a group wants money and the amount is more than a nominal amount, more like expensive commercial pricing, then I would take a second look at them.

There is always some nervousness before trying out a spiritual group and this is just ego. I remember feeling a touch nervous before I tried out the parent prayer group at my daughter's school. I reminded myself what possible threat could there be to me, for heaven's sake? If you feel unsure, don't try them, or wait till you get an urge to check them out again then feel and listen to your inner reactions.

Here's a checklist you can use:

Checklist – Litmus Test to Weed Out Cults

1.   No claims to being the only exclusive keeper or knower of the truth.

2.   No excluding or judging any individual, belief, or lack of belief.

3.   Always present positive, self-empowering ideas with no 'must do' or forms of subtle pressure.

4.   No starting you off from a position of weakness.

5.   No fear-based thinking or absolutism, or apocalyptic message.

6.   No sense of urgency or missionary zeal.

7.   No following the leader (you lead yourself).

8.   No creating dependency (like you can't do without them).

9.   No claims that if you leave the group you will lose your way spiritually.

10. No stifling of criticism or questioning or lack of open dialogue among members.

11. No suffocating or suppressed atmospheres.

12. Beware the 'guru' who feeds you fish but won't teach you *how* to fish.

13. Any negative feelings, however subtle, like flatness, nervousness, apprehension, worry, emotional mood swings – these are alarm bells.

14. No victim mind-set mentality to lure you into 'repeat business'.

The Gnostics did not pass this litmus test on a few of these indicators: They claimed to have exclusive access to the truth. There was a sense of starting you off from a position of weakness with their 108 human life limit. They did teach tools to self empower a person yet they would frame them in terms of rules. They quantified things that are not quantifiable, like saying that in our waking state we are 97 percent ego and only 3 percent consciousness and that you had to be rid of 50 percent of your karma to get off the Wheel of Life. How are you supposed to tell when you have reached those magic numbers?

What really sunk it for me about their credibility was their human lives limit. This was the fear-based thinking. No one could tell if they were on their 108th life or not, so there was a stifled atmosphere almost like a quiet desperation at the study centre. They would throw you fish but did not teach you how to fish. By that I mean they described how the ego works in our psyche but offered few techniques on how to improve the ratio between ego and consciousness.

Spiritual teacher and author, Susan Shumsky, studied for 20 years with the founder of Transcendental Meditation (TM), the Maharishi Mahesh Yogi. She had no special psychic talents and was 'born into a family of sceptics and atheists' yet always had a desire to communicate with God. Her own spiritual journey is a prime example of how a person can study with a cult-like organisation that has a strict hierarchy, only to branch out independently into something better.

In her book *How to Hear the Voice of God* which speaks about accessing the higher self, she recounts her time with the TM ashram and the downside of it. She was indoctrinated with the belief that TM was the only path to enlightenment and that the Maharishi is the only enlightened master. For many years she believed that TM teachers and practitioners were more evolved and superior than the mass of people who dwelt far outside the gates of the insulated TM community. She was climbing the hierarchy of the TM organisation when an encounter with a stranger changed everything.

She met a man at a TM community party who tried to convince her that he had something to teach her, a meditation technique that was different from the one the TM teachers were using. She scoffed at the idea and fobbed him off. Not long after this encounter she received a call from a member of the TM executive board. Someone had told the board that Susan had recently organised a New Age psychic fair in the county which was an infraction of the rules. All TM teachers are banned from any spiritual activity that was not officially sanctioned by the board. She was to appear in front of the board to explain her actions.

Practically terrified, and feeling that her spiritual future was at stake, she tracked down the man she met and disregarded at the TM party. He listened to her predicament. Then he dictated to her over the phone the affirmation and said she should repeat it for 15 minutes before facing the board. Susan was so intimidated, that she repeated it aloud for 30 minutes. Suddenly she seemed to tap into a reserve of inner strength and her fear backed down a lot.

She entered the office calmly, and instead of being met with 'glowering men ready to pounce on me', she found 'four puppy dogs' who were uncharacteristically polite. The meeting ended in her favour and the crisis seemed to evaporate.

The affirmation is given in her books *Divine Revelation* and *How to Hear the Voice of God* and is called the Self-Authority Affirmation.[43] I have used it in situations that tested my confidence and it does work.

So How to Be Discerning?

It's mostly a state of mind and attitude, but in summary, if you cultivate the following strengths you can develop a highly reliable BS detector:

- be open minded to consider other possibilities (dialectic approach)
- remember truth can be subjective and objective
- pay attention to your intuition, gut feeling, and

urges
- be as non-judgmental as possible
- don't worry about making mistakes
- go with your early impressions, feelings, or hunches – especially if they feel strong and decisive.

Finding Genuine Spiritual Books

Using the internet to research is not like going in blind. Don't be put off by internet detractors. Sure there is a lot of hogwash and personal rubbish out there, just as there is questionable quality in television and the movie industry. At least the internet has many sources of different persuasions, and for once *you* can be the information gatekeeper.

There are forums like Amazon where you can check customer reviews of a book. You can read the full spectrum of these reviews to see which ones weigh in more, the 5 star or the 1 star reviews. Don't just rely on the overall star rating on the Amazon list of titles displayed after you enter your search. This can be skewed by friends and relatives who post many favourable reviews creating a ranking that doesn't reflect the true spread of the reviews. Also, there are some people with an axe to grind so not all reviews are helpful, but those ones clearly stand out among the well-considered and fair-minded reviews.

When a book seems to have the ring of truth to it, then it is right for you. It will communicate spiritual concepts in a way that you can relate to personally. It may speak to your heart's desire, or take an approach that just clicks with your sensibilities. Unlike religion, it is not about 'one size fits all'.

Even the Dalai Lama has said that one should only follow Buddhism if it feels right for them.

Barbara Whitfield says in her book *Spiritual Awakenings*:

> 'Our best guide to all of this is our personal inner voice. As we travel our individual journeys, our inner life will become clearer and that subtle voice stronger. Read and learn from all available teachers and guides, but keep only the knowledge and information that rings true for you. Throw away the rest.'

There are spiritual books written by people who say they are sourced from channelled higher beings. Once again, rely on your BS detector. I was leery at this type of information but I have found from my personal research that there are a few genuine ones like the American 20th century psychic, Edgar Cayce, and modern channellers like Sanaya Roman. I found the books from Sanaya Roman to be helpful, loving and non-judgmental.

Discerning Real Psychic Ability

In the 19th and 20th centuries the acclaimed channellers like Edgar Cayce and the founder of Theosophy, Madame Blavatsky, would go into a trance state to channel spirits. It would appear as though they were taken over by the spirit. Today's channellers are able to channel spirit guides from a normal conscious state. They 'tune in' rather than go into a trance. Due to our better understanding of human psychology and the psyche, the consciousness no longer needs to be bypassed.

If you visit a psychic or medium today and they channel in a trance state and use a different voice, I would be wary. They may well be channelling an astral entity that is not spiritual. You can also tell their sincerity by the things that are said. There should be no grandiose statements and no fortune-telling. Because we operate from free will and choice at every moment, it is not possible to predict the future with accuracy. A true psychic will tell you what you *need* to hear, not what you *want* to hear.

In Susan Shumsky's book, *Divine Revelation*, she warns of self-appointed prophets, great spirits, gurus, and channelling in general and says this about indiscriminate channelling:

> 'Misguided people believe that mediums are somehow special, with gifts ordinary people do not possess. These anointed few may believe themselves to be the only ones capable of contacting higher beings, calling themselves the accredited messengers, or similar drivel.'

Be aware there are border-line spiritual teachers/authors. One of them is the late Elizabeth Clare Prophet who published many constructive spiritual self-help books. She claimed to be the only one or an 'accredited' messenger for the Ascended Masters. Apparently later in life, her ego overshadowed her and some followers found themselves in a state of obedience to her. This is why being discerning is important so you can still benefit from the wisdoms they have been entrusted to share, just don't get caught up in the cult of guru personality. They are still human, just like you. Don't let others make decisions for you. Always accept responsibility for yourself by realising you have a choice in every aspect.

In the early stage of my spiritual journey, I was not confident of my ability to make the right decisions in the face of personal challenges. One of these times was when I came to a cross-roads in my occupational life. It was then I decided to see a psychic for the first time ever. I decided to go for fun, like a parlour game just to lighten my mood. I would go along with it, serious face, just for the spooky candle-lit atmosphere but with my tongue planted firmly in my cheek. I responded to an impulse that gently persisted and I followed my intuition when I chose the psychic.

Fortunately for me, the psychic I chose turned out to be the real thing. This took me completely by surprise. I thought it was a simple fact that all psychics were by definition charlatans. It took me a quite a while to recover from the revelation that there is such a thing as real psychic ability.

She asked me if I was wearing any metal jewellery. I gave her one of my gold rings which she held in her hands to 'tune into' her spirit guides but she did not go into a trance state. She was matter-of-fact the whole time, like it was an everyday thing for her. There was no quivering or using a different voice, and she didn't close her eyes.

During the session, I was spoken to as though I was known. It was not what I expected at all, it was very personal. There were no judgments and it was all helpful. Specific things that were too specific to be the product of an educated guess is what really threw me. She knew nothing about me other than my name and that I was looking for any and all advice to help me make a decision about the direction of my career.

I deliberately told her no other background about myself so as not to give her any food for extrapolation. All I said was that I was at an occupational cross-roads and needed some tips or insights. The reason I am telling you this, dear reader, is that sometimes things are not what they seem. If you stumble upon a similar experience or revelation, it is very satisfying, like a detective who's found an important clue. If you do decide to see a psychic out of pure curiosity, avoid those who ask you to provide answers to ten profile questions. These psychics are getting some basic facts about you first so they can triangulate and make educated guesses to form a reading along the lines of what you want to hear, not what you need to hear.

Handling Spiritual Readiness in Your Life

I like the Buddhist saying, 'When the student is ready, the teacher will appear'. Readiness is important because it is a silent path. When the truth reveals itself to you, either in dreams, a moment of clarity in the middle of chaos, or a profound feeling of love, it's a dawning that you can't easily share with others.

When you take up spiritual growth outside organised religion, it can seem lonely at first in the sense that your family and friends may not see things the way you do. You may get mixed reactions from them if you do talk about it. Most of the important people in your life are not ready themselves, in the spiritual sense. If you grew up with a strong ethnic family religion, it can feel like you are going out on a limb.

It is possible to discuss spirituality within the bounds of a person's comfort zone. I don't discuss it much with my parents as it doesn't accord with their way of thinking. Even though my mother left the Catholic faith to become Anglican, my step-father is involved with the synod and they attend church every Sunday and enjoy the fellowship with their local community. I have touched upon some spiritual themes with them, in a broad sense, but stop as soon as they look uncomfortable.

They don't believe I've gone off track (or maybe they do), it's just that they prefer their way of understanding and appreciating God. They can see that I am a caring and responsible person so they are not concerned that I don't attend church or belong to a religion. Sometimes I will talk with them about Jesus, like his two great commandments, his humility, and how he practiced what he preached. But I don't drive the point home that the crucifixion of Jesus was not to save us from our sins but to set an example of being Christ-like.

My husband is an atheistic scientist/engineer of Jewish origin. I don't discuss spirituality with him except Buddhist concepts. I refer to the power of being in the now, positive thinking, and mutually appreciating the majesty of nature. I suggest the Buddhist wisdom of detachment when he is confronted with something unpleasant, but I don't let him know that in my opinion 'turn the other cheek' is more spiritually evolved than 'eye for an eye'. Once I couldn't help myself and said to him 'It's time to look beyond the numbers' and he cried, 'More numbers!'

If you've been brought up with a traditional religion that binds your family, you can seek higher spiritual truths and not have it overturn your life. I say this because many people fear that to become spiritual in a life-changing sense would mean walking away from your established religion and changing things in your life to meet the dictates of the spiritual teaching. The great spiritual teachers in the past, like Jesus, Buddha and Gandhi, who advocated walking away from your family and authority structures, did so because in those days authority had more direct control over a person's self-determination. Authority and convention were more absolute and were imposed on the individual without question.

Unless you are in a setting that conflicts with spiritual values like doing a job you hate (and it may be killing you inside), most settings in a person's life can be leveraged for spiritual growth, even living in a dysfunctional family. To make the most of what you already have, and to cultivate the good side, is less risky than changing your circumstances to suit some high spiritual ideal. Otherwise you could sew the seed for a backlash later down the track if things don't meet this ideal.

Letting go of the need to control and surrendering to fully trust the process will make life better than you could possibly imagine. I am constantly amazed by the creative imagination of Spirit - it leaves me for dead. I found that I didn't have to agonise over the things in my life I wanted to change because as I grew spiritually, those things changed by themselves as a natural outflow of my inner change.

At times the change in you might mean you lose interest in something you did with another, and this might upset them. Dealing with their reaction can be seen as a spiritual challenge to handle it with understanding and patience. You could offer an alternative activity to do together that suits your new sensibilities. Remember that true spirituality, in essence, is anti-nothing and includes all, so becoming more spiritual should not cause any distancing between yourself and another person, unless you choose it. On the contrary, you come to tolerate people's differences with an open mind and more compassion, and can stand their annoying traits more easily. You become less judgemental and don't mind trying to see the good in them.

As Joel Goldsmith says about keeping your relationship with God:

> 'Do not be concerned about your relationships with people. Consciously maintain your relationship with God, and this will take care of everything else. Keep your realisation of your relationship with God sacred and secret. This relationship, maintained in silence and secrecy, appears as harmonious human relationships and experiences.'

Others in your life may ask questions about spirituality that are difficult to answer because they are too broad, or seem to be the wrong question. A family member or friend may ask you a broad question like, 'Tell me about spirituality'. This type of question can't be answered easily on the spot so you could ask them to be more specific. What aspect are they curious about? Notice how the question is asked. Does the person seem sincere or does it seem like they are baiting you into an argument. The way a question is asked, and when it is asked, will reveal a lot about the sincerity of the person.

If they can't be specific, you can say it's about self-improvement, guiding your energies into effortless action through the use of meditation, mantras, developing self-awareness, and transforming the ego to be your servant, not your master. You can't be more specific than that because you'd end up lecturing the person. It is self-paced and best acquired layer by layer. It's not that you are being guarded, you are giving them as much information as they can process at that point. Leave it to your intuition to know when and what to say. If not sure, pause and take a deep breath before answering.

You may get questions from your children, especially if they see you are devoting a set amount of time to meditation every day. It's wonderful to have a child who is naturally curious and is not afraid to ask questions. When my pre-teen daughter asked me and I couldn't reply simply, I told her, 'Just be a child for now and save those questions for later.' A child's mind is a mysterious thing and I didn't want to overtake her natural development. I said to her that I would save my materials for when she grows up and that if she's interested she can take up her own spiritual quest. She asked me, what if she doesn't. I replied that's fine too.

If you are tempted to convince others or get them interested, the best way is to show, not tell. You can only spark their curiosity but you can't convince them of anything. Ultimately, all will come to the truth in their own time, in their own way because otherwise it would be forced, unnatural and not genuine. If it's not really from the heart, the curiosity would only be fleeting.

If a friend asks me about spirituality, the first and only thing I point to is the power of being in the moment. This is constructive and helpful because the foundation for growing spiritually is living in the now. Many people these days are familiar with that wisdom so it's a good starting point. Unless someone asks you a specific question, it is better to be and do, than say. I tried to encourage a friend who suffers depression and hit a wall with her. She seemed curious, yet she was not curious. I had to let the whole discourse drop, much as I would have liked to help her.

On the importance of show not tell, Jeni told me that her husband was dealing with strong emotions over stress at work. She said that he noticed her transformation recently and her ability to handle her family dynamics more effectively. He asked her how she was able to 'transform [her] personality like that'. It was the first time he asked a question like this but his question was so broad, she felt unable to answer it. She said:

> 'I don't know just how serious he is, or how passionate he is. I think he is just frustrated with the way he is feeling and wants to know how to get rid of it. He listens to a meditation CD everyday, which is helping.'

I suggested she ask him how he feels when he gets these feelings and go from there. Depending on the response, your intuition can guide you.

Most people have friends or family members who have no interest in spirituality or religion at all, and still hold to the view that religion has caused so many wars in the world that it must be bad or delusional. Such a person might confront you when they see you are spending more time on an activity which is a break from the usual routine. This could be your commitment to meditate every day or going to an esoteric talk instead of doing zumba twice a week. The best thing is to refuse to get drawn into an argument with them over justifying yourself. Show grace at all times.

They might say, 'It's rubbish.'

You could respond, 'Then it will come to nothing so what are you worried about?'

They might reply, 'Because it's all too easy to delude people.'

You could say, 'Yeah, I noticed.'

Spiritual growth is a life-long journey to gain more of what you want or aspire to be, and, to know the difference between what is permanent and what is temporary. It is growing into something, slowly, finding a new respect for the status quo in your life and working with these things, not against them, seeing them as vehicles for your learning and growth. It doesn't matter if your family members are dogmatically religious or hard-boiled atheists. Maybe the makeup of your family is that way to teach you about respecting people's differences. I know mine is.

The most recent spiritual wisdom says you can forge your own path because we are capable of it now that we live in an information age and knowledge is more accessible. For the first time in history a person can readily acquire information about anything, except something that involves national security or 'commercial in confidence', of course.

There are Buddhist holistic health centres that hold meditation sessions and teachers of spiritual disciplines like yoga, reiki or tai chi, for example. If you live in a remote area, or the nearest spiritual or holistic centre is hundreds of miles away, there are many online courses you can find by searching the internet. You can order books online and have them delivered to your door.

I was reading a discussion forum at the Nickelodeon Parents Connect website on the question 'What do all religions have in common'. One visitor in the Comments area said:

> 'I am first and foremost Catholic. I have also adopted some Buddhism and Hinduism into my thinking as well. But I adopt the principles that they all hold.'

So there you go. As you continue your spiritual search and practice the tools consistently over a period of time, you will experience synchronicities and moments of Spirit touching your life. The only way others can see any sign of your spiritual awakening is that outwardly, you seem more at peace and are easier to get along with.

Enjoying the Fruits of Your Higher Self

You arrive at the point when your ego no longer tries to sabotage your efforts at self improvement. You may switch between ego and higher self because you are consciously aware of the difference. So much so that you can stop yourself from a full-blown ego reaction, which may still be your default, but with a difference. There is a split second of a window of time where, if you are fast enough, you can choose to seek inspiration from your higher self before you react. If you have been open-minded and in a balanced frame of mind all day you probably will react with your higher self anyway.

Operating through the higher self means you are far less affected by the negative acts of other people. If you are affected, your anger is on your outer edge and doesn't rip through you. You become more patient with other people's shortcomings and less disturbed by their failings. It's easier to see the opportunity for growth that challenging people and circumstances present, even if you are not entirely happy about it.

This is the fruits of the surrendered ego. It no longer feels under threat by your determination to grow and is willing to take a back-seat to your higher self at the steering wheel. The ego's new ability to relax, or relinquish control to you, is slowly raising its vibration and transmuting its traits into the corresponding virtues.

An everyday evidence of this would be when someone is rude or inconsiderate toward you. Instead of taking offence, you find you are not taking it personally. Instead of being irritated, you may find yourself feeling tolerance for the person. It doesn't seem like a big deal but this is a monumental shift in your being.

Overall, what becomes increasingly obvious over time is that what used to bother you no longer does, or you see it as being smaller, transitory and less important than you used to regard it. If there is something in your life you are not entirely pleased with you can sense quite easily that it's not the be all and end all.

When you spend more time as your higher self, you become more creative and purposeful. You have more physical energy and you don't need as much sleep to function well. Your centre of balance improves so that if you slip on something, it's much easier to recover. You don't fall like a sack of potatoes because you are lighter in your body.

At some time you may be tempted to force your ego into an uncomfortable situation just to bring it out into the open. But be careful that your ego doesn't see this as an ambush. This is what happened to me once when I tried to outsmart myself. I decided to include an extended family member to a dinner invitation who I didn't really want to see. I have an ego reaction to this person who rubs me the wrong way.

I reasoned that perhaps they feel the same way about me. For all I know I could be giving negative vibes through my body language, tone of voice, and facial expressions. When they pick this up in me, it would trigger similar feelings towards me. I then pick up their negative reaction to my projection, and instead of realising they are reacting to my negativity, my ego would declare that my feelings towards this person are vindicated. What a recipe for perpetual tension, even animosity between people.

I had decided to test myself, but at the last minute my plan derailed and not only was the person not able to make it, but the whole arrangement was off. It felt like I was off the hook but the next day something triggered a loud argument between myself and my husband. As usual it was petty, and as usual I was caught off guard and it wasn't until I was well into the argument that I realised my ego was riding me like a pony (again).

I wanted to tell you this because from practicing self awareness you can learn so much about yourself. There was one problem with my so-called great idea. When we are tested by the universe it is always when we least expect it. There is no way to anticipate the challenge, so the surprise factor not only tests our sincerity but how far we have come. For this reason my planned testing of my ego fizzled out. It really would have been no test at all because I was prepared.

As you come to fully realize that no-one outside yourself can actually control how you feel and think, you can let this sink in slowly as the rational mind can't make sense of it. You can be disappointed by a person's behavior or decision, but it will not bring you down to a point of sadness or depression. This attitude, not depending on external events to make or break your happiness, can become a default way of being that grows stronger over time. Life becomes a whole lot easier and more pleasurable.

Of course you can't constantly police your thoughts and emotions, so no matter how far you have come there will be days when you feel less up-beat. If I feel flat, I try not to feed it. I even accept it. I feel that there's a reason to be feeling flat on this particular day. The last thing you want to do is to get overly self-conscious of feelings you don't want.

The more often you are your higher self, the less opportunity your ego has to run you and take over completely. It becomes less compelling and easier to resist. You develop resiliency and are able to easily withstand life challenges without going through immobilising fear and anxiety attacks. The intellectual part of your mind gets clearer, being less cluttered by emotion in general so you can muster the self discipline to apply yourself to anything whenever you decide.

Your self awareness does get tested now and then. There may be an unanticipated event that catches you unaware, trips you up, or presses a hot button. Suddenly you are in the moment, but not in a spiritual sense. Your ego is centre stage reacting to the event and you are dealing with emotional reflex, and not all of it positive. These types of occurrences can throw you. But don't worry, it is only temporary. Just be sure to resume your higher ways of being when the drama has settled.

In Dick Sutphen's book, *The Spiritual Path Guidebook*, he points out that:

> 'Anytime you are upset with someone else, it is a self-created Karmic test to see how much you've learned and whether you'll need to be tested in the future. If you responded with love, non-judgement, compassion or neutrality, you probably passed the test.'

Remember in spirituality it's never too late. Don't think you failed because you didn't react the way you hoped, even if this happened ten times already. You were probably caught off guard, completely, and it is very hard to intercept an emotional reaction when you are upset by another. Know that you may be tested like this again, but the next time, you are better prepared. Next time you will pass because of the prep work with this incident.

About a year into our shared spiritual journey, Jeni and I were predicting that our egos would not like what we were doing and that a revolt would occur, an uprising, even an ego attack. Now because we both anticipated it with a sense of logical certainty, we gave it legs and it actually happened.

Jeni fractured a bone in her ankle from a bad land during a Ninjitsu lesson, and became depressed due to her incapacitation. At the same time, I was fighting off a blanket of negativity that had descended on me after a frustrating disappointment over a work opportunity, that had all the promising signs in the beginning, but went pear shaped (the story told in the Case Study).

To spare yourself a major drama in your life, I strongly recommend that you do not think about, or anticipate, a backlash from your ego. Don't let such an idea take root in your mind at all, for any reason. At the time, we did not realize what we were doing and probably thought it was something to expect because we are so used to duality thinking.

Even though we already knew about not fighting the ego, we would refer to our spiritual work as 'battling the ego' and 'struggling with ego'. Remember the basic principles of the Law of Attraction, whatever you spend most of your time thinking about you will attract into your life. The moral of the story is - don't analyse or define your efforts too much. If it does seem like a struggle in the early days, don't pay attention to the struggle. Just focus on the doing, the awareness and the sincerity.

It is not necessary to suffer in order to learn and grow. We have evolved enough to gain the ability to keep ego at arms length, and work with it to integrate it into our whole Self. The key to training the ego is not to think in terms of 'conquering', 'battle' or 'struggle'. This will create a duality – me versus it. The ego thrives on opposition and struggle, and so you would only entrench it. This was the downfall of the Gnostic approach and I saw long-term followers who always seemed quiet. They appeared to me like they had hit a wall with their spiritual growth.

The bottom line is that it's not about constantly striving, heaving effort, it is more about desire, will, sincerity and readiness. When you have all these facets awake in you, your growth becomes boosted. What brings on the awakening within you? Choice you make. When you decide you want to know what's behind life and why we are here, then you are indeed awakened.

We can now learn and grow through joy. You will experience feelings that words can't describe, sublime highly pleasant feelings that come from Love. Once you reach a certain stage of growth and awakening you won't want to go back to ego dominating, because what it offers is vastly inferior. Its sameness, negative antics, false urgency, and ridiculous fears, all fail to hypnotise you anymore.

As you grow, your dream life gets richer and you will get message dreams from time to time. These are not the majority of dreams which are replays of your day or what's currently concerning you. These never last in your memory anyway, even if you do recall them. I am talking about the dreams you never forget. I remember my early dreams would sometimes have me in the grounds of an amusement park (a dream metaphor for the illusory life of the ego). Now I have a different backdrop like a gymnasium, or a school, which gives me the message that I am working out, building strength. It's encouraging.

Spiritual growth is the most individual thing you can possibly imagine. It is meant to develop and optimise your uniqueness because God wants to experience, through us, in every way imaginable. So you can see there is no place for sameness, and the ego's way which seeks control, authority and conformity.

All the exercises in this book can be modified to suit your sensibilities. It's as fun, or as hard work, as you make it. You don't have to follow suggestions in self-help books to the letter. Most of the authors will tell you they are giving examples and samples, and by all means be your own artist in the canvas of your life, make your own brush strokes.

Remember, you don't have to find the time or substitute one activity for another. Any situation in life can be a vehicle for your efforts to work on ego. It can be as simple as starting to look at things differently. Using certain situations to improve your self awareness, being in the moment, and taking a deep breath before immediately reacting. This might not sound like much but it's quite powerful and far reaching.

Rushing your development or striving with all your might to do it right, is not what its about. Be patient with your ego's pace, resistance and initial attempts at sabotage. Once you observe yourself more and make it a habit you can steer yourself in the direction you want to go. Don't bog yourself down with self-judgements along the way; it's a waste of energy.

You don't need to believe or have faith in what this book is telling you. Until you try some of the suggestions and exercises yourself, it's just theory and the author's personal experiences. What excites me, as author of this book, is that as you read these words now you are taking my word for it, or feeling that you are. But wait till you come to the same conclusion I did but in your own special way, unique to you. As Jill Shinn says 'There is nothing more exhilarating and magical than following the path of Spirit'.

Postscript:

I spent a few days with Jeni when I visited the US in 2011 to attend a wedding in Palm Springs. She flew up from New Mexico and we stayed at the same hotel in Los Angeles. We were looking forward to meeting face to face after corresponding over the internet for so long and sending photos of each other. She was tall like me, and slender, with fair skin and naturally curly and fading strawberry blonde hair.

Each morning we frequented a café for breakfast, called Danny's Diner. I'm told this is a very ordinary family diner but it was better in LA than anywhere else I have tried it so we were happy to go there for a cheap feed. There was a waiter there who habitually served us and we would chat pleasantries with him. He looked to be in his early 60s, was average height and slender build with brown eyes and hair. His voice had a pleasant patient tone and his face indicated to me he was a sensitive type with humble ambitions. He seemed to be one of those people who is satisfied with what he has and doesn't need to prove anything or strive for more, even though I thought he should be retired from an occupation like waiting at a restaurant.

One day he surprised us with his own take on spirituality when he saw a Dick Sutphen book Jeni was reading that she had placed on the table. He was of that mind-set that can be suspicious of new age spirituality and said he reads 'only the Scriptures'. Even so, he had his own take on the Bible that was quite creative at times. He told us about his own personal connection to God, that he regularly becomes aware of God's presence when he's having a shower. He would ask Spirit why do you always come to me when I'm washing myself? At one point he talked about lost human souls with the deep sadness of a parent who faces losing one of their children to crime. He spoke about his faith with such conviction and depth of heart, that we were nearly moved to tears. I was speechless and humbled and Jeni's eyes were watery.

The next day when we came to the café we felt a bit self conscious and looked around for the waiter. There he was, and he came to our table to serve us again. He continued to speak to us about spirituality. But this time something was off. What he was saying didn't have the same ring of truth to it. We politely listened but we weren't moved by what he was saying.

I cherish that experience because we met his higher self who inspired us, and the next day, his ego self that left us feeling flat. It made me appreciate just how much ego needs to be understood.

THE END (or The Beginning).

Notes

Chapter 1 – The Starting Point

1. Australian Broadcasting Corporation, *First Wednesday (5/11/1997) – Has the Church Lost its Way?*, TV Program Sales, VHS video, ©1997.

2. Population Census (Australia): *The National Church Life Survey* is affiliated with the Australian National Census and was started in 1991 (a census year) when churches became interested in watching the changing landscape of faith and church attendance. It measures church attendance every five years.
(viewed August 2013) http://www.ncls.org.au/,

3. Prof. Elaine Pagels, *The Gnostic Gospels*, Penguin Books, 1990

4. Integral Yoga of Sri Aurobindo & The Mother, *Difference between religion and spirituality*, (viewed August 2013), http://auromere.wordpress.com/2010/01/24/difference-between-religion-and-spirituality/

Chapter 2 – The Ego Self

5. Carl Gustav Jung, *The Structure of the Psyche, The Structure and Dynamics of the Psyche*, (Collected Works of C.G. Jung, Volume 8), C. G. Jung (Author), Gerhard Adler (Translator), Princeton University Press, 2nd ed., 1972.

6. Susan Shumsky, *Divine Revelation*, Fireside Books (Simon & Schuster Inc.), 1996.

7. Michael Newton Ph.D, *Journey of Souls: Case Studies of Life Between Lives*, Llewellyn Publications, 1994.

8.   Belzebuub, *The Peace of the Spirit Within- A guide to transform your life*, Absolute Publishing Group, 2006.

9.   Adrian P. Cooper, *Our Ultimate Reality – Life, the Universe and Destiny of Mankind*, Ultimate Reality Publishing, November 2007.

10. Jerry Hirschfield, *My Ego, My Higher Power and I – A Transformational Journey from Ego to Higher self*, HI Productions, California, 2nd ed., 1991.

Chapter 3 – Ego Anatomy

11. Ancient and Future Catholics, *The Seven Deadly Sins*, (viewed March 2012) http://www.ancient-future.net/catholiclists.html

12. Mark L. Prophet, Elizabeth Clare Prophet, *The Masters and Their Retreats*, Summit University Press, January 2003.

13. *Samael Aun Weor* – Largely unknown in the English-speaking world, he was born in 1917 in Columbia as Victor Rodriguez and was founder of the Universal Christian Gnostic Movement. He was passionate about gnosis and once said, 'Do not follow me. I am just a signpost. Reach your own self-realization.' There are websites devoted to debunking this man which are as numerous as the historical factual websites on this branch of Gnosticism. (Source at Glorian Publishing (non-profit org) at http://www.samaelaunweor.info/ (viewed December 2014)

14. Glorian Publishing, *What are the three brains and five centres?*, Gnostic Teachings, (viewed December 2014), http://gnosticteachings.org/the-teachings-of-gnosis/resources-and-references/815-three-brains-and-five-centers.html

15. Jim Meskauskas, *Thesis—Antithesis--Synthesis*, Clickz – Marketing News & Expert Advice, http://www.clickz.com/clickz/column/1703443/thesis-antithesis-synthesis, November 6, 2001 (viewed March 2014).

16. Remez Sasson, *Mind Your Mind – Articles about Mind Power*, self-published free e-book, 2007, sourced: http://www.successconsciousness.com

17. Barbara Harris Whitfield, *Spiritual Awakenings – Insights of the NDE and Other Doorways to Our Soul*, Health Communications Inc, 1995.

18.   Martin Seligman, *Authentic Happiness: Using the New Positive Psychology*, The Free Press (division of Simon & Schuster), 2002.

Chapter 4 – Ego Psychology

19. Allan Hardman's Toltec Apprentice Community Online, *Toltec Wisdom - The Toltecs of Ancient Mexico*, http://tolteconline.com/ (viewed May 2014).

20. Don Miguel Ruiz & Don Jose Ruiz, *The Fifth Agreement – A practical guide to self-mastery*, Amber-Allen Publishing, 2010.

21. Jerry Hirschfield, *My Ego, My Higher Power and I – A Transformational Journey from Ego to Higher self*, HI Productions, California, 2nd ed., 1991.

Chapter 5 – Ego in Training

22. Dr Joshua David Stone, *How to Release Fear-Based Thinking and Feeling - An Indepth Study of Spiritual Psychology*, Vol 2, Writers Club Press, 2001

23. Remez Sasson, *Your Mind – Mind Articles about Mind Power*, e-book, 2007, http://www.successconsciosness.com.

Chapter 7 – Mentoring the Ego

24. Marvin Meyer, *The Gospel of Thomas – The Hidden Sayings of Jesus*, HarperSanFrancisco (Harper Collins), 1992.

25. Jill Shinn, Remembering *Who You Are – A Guide to Spiritual Awakening and Inner Peace*, Createspace Independent Publishing, 2011.

26. Dick Sutphen, *Lighting the Light Within*, Valley of the Sun Pub Co, May 1987.

27. Elizabeth Clare Prophet, *Access the Power of Your Higher self*, Summit University Press, 1997.

28. Daniel Dennett, *Breaking the Spell: Religion as a Natural Phenomenon*, Penguin Books; February, 2007.

29. Dr Joe Vitale, *Guidebook for The Missing Secret – How to Use the Law of Attraction to Easily Attract What You Want*, Nightingale Conant, 2008.

30. Brandon Bays, *The Journey – An Extraordinary Guide for Healing Your Life and Setting Yourself Free*, Harper Element, 1999.

31. Dr Joshua David Stone, *How to Clear the Negative Ego*, iUniverse , February 2001

32. Neale Donald Walsch, *Conversations with God – Book One*, Hachette Australia, January 1997.

Chapter 8 – Being Your Higher Self

33. Thich Nhat Hanh, *Thich Nhat Hanh: Essential Writings*, Orbis Books, 2001.

34. Elizabeth Clare Prophet, *Access The Power Of Your Higher Self (Pocket Guides to Practical Spirituality)*, Summit University Press, 1997.

35. Joel S. Goldsmith, *The Infinite Way*, DeVorss, 1947, released in paperback - Createspace, October, 2013.

36.   Mark Ellis, *Men on the Moon: Astronauts Talk About Spiritual Experieneces in a New Documentary*, 25th October, 2007, www.intheshadowofthemoon.com, (viewed December 2014).

Chapter 9 – Spiritual Readiness

37.   Joel Goldsmith, *The Infinite Way*, DeVorss, 1947.

38.   The Krishnamurti Centre, http://www.krishnamurticentre.org.uk/teachings/

39.   Jerry Hirschfield, *My Ego, My Higher Power and I – A Transformational Journey from Ego to Higher self*, HI Productions, California, 1991.

40.   Edgar Cayce, *On Channelling Your Higher Self*, by Henry Reed, Warner Books, 1989, pg 76-77.

41.   The Two Great Commandments are discussed at *Catholicity – The Catholic Church Simplified* website http://www.catholicity.com/baltimore-catechism/lesson15.html (viewed May 2014)

42.   Barbara Harris Whitfield, *Spiritual Awakenings – Insights of the NDE and Other Doorways to Our Soul*, Health Communications Inc, 1995.

43.   Susan G Shumsky, *Divine Revelation*, Simon & Schuster, 1996. Susan G Shumsky, *How to Hear the Voice of God*, New Page Books, 2008.

Bibliography (Recommended Reading)

Books

Dr Wayne W Dyer, *The Power of Intention – Learning to Co-create Your World Your Way*, Hay House, 2004.

Elizabeth Anne Hill with Catherine Mary Hill, *Twin Souls – A Message of Hope for the New Millennium*, Gateway 4 the Golden Age, August, 2007

Susan Jeffers Ph D, *Feel the Fear and Do It Anyway*, Random House Publishing Group, 1987

Anne Jones, *Healing Negative Energies*, Piatkus, 2002

Anne Jones, *The Soul Connection – How to Access Your Higher Powers and Discover Your True Self*, Piatkus, 2002

Ken Keyes Jr, *Handbook to Higher Consciousness*, Love Line Books, 1995

Kenneth James MacLean, *Dialogues – Conversations with my Higher Self*, 2005

Joseph Murphy PhD, *The Power of Your Subconscious Mind*, Simon & Schuster,1988

Michael Newton PhD, *Journey of Souls – Case Studies of Life Between Lives*, Llewellyn Publications, 2006

S. Roman, *Spiritual Growth – Be Your Higher Self*, H J Kramer, 1989

S. Roman, *Personal Power Through Awareness*, H J Kramer, 1986

C.A. Russ, Peel Away the Layers to Your Real Radiant Self, Violet Fire Productions, 2010

Jill Shinn, *Remembering Who You Are – A Guide to Spiritual Awakening and Inner Peace*, Wakeup Sweetheart Publication, 2011.

Sandy Stevenson, The Awakener – The Time is Now, Gill & Macmillan, 1997

Dr Joshua David Stone, *How to Release Fear-Based Thinking and Feeling, An Indepth Study of Spiritual Psychology – vol 2*, Writers Club Press, 2001

Recommended Articles

The Energy Healing Site, *Chakra Tones: Using Vocal Toning to Open and Balance Your Chakras*, http://www.the-energy-healing-site.com/chakra-tones.html.

Dr Stephen Diamond, *Dangerous Genius: The Rise and Fall of Phil Spector*, Psychology Today, http://www.psychologytoday.com/blog/evil-deeds/201303/dangerous-genius-the-rise-and-fall-phil-spector, 2013.

Stephen A. Diamond, Ph.D. (forensic psychologist), *Essential Secrets of Psychotherapy: What is the "Shadow"? - Understanding the "dark side" of our psyche*, Psychology Today, http://www.psychologytoday.com/blog/evil-deeds/201204/essential-secrets-psychotherapy-what-is-the-shadow, 2012

Heart Compass Enterprises, Metaphysics-for-life.com, *Heart Intelligence is a higher level of intelligence that supports physical, mental and emotional well being*, (viewed February 2015), http://www.metaphysics-for-life.com/heart-intelligence.html

Thom Markham, *Heart, Brain and Intelligence*, ASCD Edge – Professional Networking Community for Educators, (viewed February 2015)

http://edge.ascd.org/_Heart-Brain-and-
Intelligence/blog/3455546/127586.html

Steve Robertson, Huffington Post Healthy Living, *Mindfulness and the Monkey Mind* http://www.huffingtonpost.com/steve-robertson/mindfulness_b_3422820.html

Essay on the relationship between Freud and Jung and development of personality theory - http://www.criminology.fsu.edu/crimtheory/jung/jung.html

Kendra Cherry, *Jung's Archetypes*, Psychology About.com, http://psychology.about.com/od/personalitydevelopment/tp/archetypes.htm

Sources on Gnosticism

For the difference between the Lost Gnostic Gospels and the Dead Sea Scrolls see The Gnostic Society Library –. http://gnosis.org/library/dss/dss.htm

For a history of Gnosticism and the Orthodox Christian Church see, Christian Apologetics and Research Ministry, http://carm.org/heresy.

www.ingramcontent.com/pod-product-compliance
Lightning Source LLC
Chambersburg PA
CBHW060251100426
42742CB00011B/1712